Guidelines for the Preparation of Teachers of English Language Arts

1996 Edition

NCTE Standing Committee on Teacher Preparation and Certification

Chair: Robert C. Small Jr., Radford University

Attitudes Subcommittee
Chair: Jacqueline Bryant-Turner, McDougal Littell, Virginia Beach
June Langford Berkley, Ohio University
James M. Brewbaker, Columbus College
Rosentene B. Purnell, California State University-Northridge

Knowledge Subcommittee
Chair: Lenora (Leni) Cook, California State University-Dominguez Hills
Michael Angelotti, University of Oklahoma
Wendell Schwartz, Adlai E. Stevenson High School
Charles Joseph Thomas, Bergen Community College
Robert A. Tremmel, Iowa State University
Marcia Venegas-García, University of California-San Diego

Pedagogy Subcommittee
Chair: William H. Peters, Texas A&M University
Patricia P. Kelly, Virginia Tech
Frieda M. Owen, Wood County Schools, West Virginia
Karen Schuster Webb, University of Kentucky

Interrelations among the Guidelines Subcommittee
Chair: Frieda M. Owen, Wood County Schools, West Virginia
Michael Angelotti, University of Oklahoma
Amy A. McClure, Ohio Wesleyan University

Relation to Standards Projects Subcommittee
Chair: Charles Joseph Thomas, Chair, Bergen Community College
Mildred C. Melendez, Sinclair Community College
Rosentene B. Purnell, California State University-Northridge

Effective Teacher-Preparation Programs Subcommittee
Chair: James M. Brewbaker, Chair, Columbus College
June Langford Berkley, Ohio University
Karen Schuster Webb, University of Kentucky

Transition to Teaching Subcommittee
Chair: Patricia P. Kelly, Chair, Virginia Tech
Marcia Venegas-García, University of California-San Diego

Continuing Issues Subcommittee
Chair: Robert A. Tremmel, Chair, Iowa State University
Jacqueline Bryant-Turner, McDougal Littell, Virginia Beach
Lenora (Leni) Cook, California State University-Dominguez Hills
William H. Peters, Texas A&M University

NCTE Staff Liaison: Sandra E. Gibbs

Guidelines for the Preparation of Teachers of English Language Arts

1996 Edition

Prepared by
Robert C. Small Jr., Chair,
and
Members of NCTE's Standing Committee on Teacher Preparation and Certification

Endorsed by
NCTE's Executive Committee, February 1996

NCTE National Council of Teachers of English
1111 W. Kenyon Road, Urbana, Illinois 61801-1096

Editor: Michelle Sanden Johlas
Cover Design: Joellen Bryant
Interior Design: Michael Getz

NCTE Stock Number 19808-3050

Library of Congress Cataloging-in-Publication Data

Guidelines for the preparation of teachers of English language arts / National Council of Teachers of English ; prepared by NCTE's Standing Committee on Teacher Preparation and Certification, Robert C. Small Jr., Chair. — 1996 ed.

    p.   cm.

  "Endorsed by NCTE's Executive Committee, February 1996."

  ISBN 0-8141-1980-8 (pbk.)

  1. English teachers—Training of—Standards—United States. 2. Language arts teachers—Training of—Standards—United States.   I. Small, Robert C. II. NCTE Standing Committee on Teacher Preparation and Certification. III. National Council of Teachers of English.

PE1068.U5G8   1996

428'.007—dc20   96-43165

CONTENTS

02-17-06 um

Acknowledgments

Every ten years, the National Council of Teachers of English issues an official set of guidelines for programs that prepare teachers of the English language arts. This document represents a new set of such guidelines, built upon those published in 1986.

Three years ago the NCTE Standing Committee on Teacher Preparation and Certification met at the NCTE Spring Conference in Richmond, Virginia, and began to make a series of not-always-easy decisions that led to this set of guidelines. (But the revision process had begun years earlier with the work of Denny Wolfe, chair of the committee that prepared the 1986 guidelines. It was continued and developed further by Gillian Cook, chair of the Standing Committee from 1987 through 1992.) We were determined to build statements about teacher education on the wisdom and insights of a wide cross section of NCTE members. To this end, members of the committee volunteered to act as liaisons to various sections, conferences, commissions, standing committees, committees, and assemblies of the Council. The NCTE leaders responded with ideas, suggestions, and criticisms that have helped our work immeasurably. We thank each of them.

Our Standing Committee also decided to divide itself into three subcommittees to explore the three areas of emphasis (knowledge, pedagogy, and attitudes) in the 1986 guidelines and to consider whether the 1996 guidelines should be organized around the same three broad areas of teacher preparation. Three long-term members of the committee were chosen to chair these subcommittees. Jacqueline Bryant-Turner, Leni Cook, and Bill Peters guided the work of each subcommittee and communicated by mail, fax, phone, and e-mail at a furious rate. All this hard work resulted in a meeting during a warm July in Urbana, at which we conceptualized the current document; we also met almost nonstop during two NCTE Annual Conventions. No *Guidelines* would exist without the dedication and vigilance of these three members.

Sandra E. Gibbs, the committee's NCTE liaison, both kept us on track and brought to our work her extensive experience and understanding of research and best practice in the preparation of teachers of English language arts. She supplied documents that brought us up to date on the work of the many standards projects that had an impact on our work, and she kept us informed about the developments within the National Council for the Accreditation of Teacher Education, the International Reading Association, and other national organizations that influence teacher preparation. She brought us together at that July meeting in Urbana, helped us think through the issues, and participated in the discussions, analyses, and debates that marked that meeting. Without her, we might still be examining the issues rather than celebrating the publication of the 1996 *Guidelines*.

A special friend of the committee is Delores Lipscomb. Though not a member of the committee—and we tried to persuade her to accept membership despite her other major commitments—she joined us for that meeting in Urbana, sharing her insights into teacher preparation and her expertise on teaching in urban settings. Her influence is clear in every aspect of these *Guidelines*.

I personally owe a special debt to Patricia Kelly and James Brewbaker, who served as an editing team for the final draft of the *Guidelines*. They eliminated jargon, redundancies, and ponderous sentences, and the *Guidelines* improved in readability and style under their figurative red pens.

A special thanks also goes to Larry Crapse, English coordinator for School District One in Florence, South Carolina. Although he is not a member of the Standing Committee, he offered us the insight of his experiences as a new teacher. His reflections illuminate both what preservice teacher education can do and what, in the end, is beyond its scope.

There are, of course, others who critiqued parts of this document, who dropped by our committee meetings and program sessions at NCTE conferences, and who spoke with us during breaks at NCTE general sessions to provide us with ideas and sometimes to insist that we look carefully at this issue or that problem. We have, no doubt, pleased a few and disappointed some others. But even if our revision of the *Guidelines* does not satisfy all who helped us, we do thank you and reassure you that we thought carefully about every suggestion that you took the time to share with us.

Robert C. Small Jr., Chair
NCTE Standing Committee on Teacher Preparation and Certification

Introduction

At ten-year intervals for most of its eighty-five years, the National Council of Teachers of English has presented the profession with a statement of what effective teachers of the English language arts need to know and be able to do; these regularly updated statements also discuss the attitudes that effective teachers should possess. In many ways each decade's guidelines give us a fascinating look at the time's prevailing philosophies regarding what students should learn and how they should be taught. The documents also reflect the changing views about the role of teachers and schools in general. In addition, of course, these statements reveal changing ideas about how teachers should be prepared.

These periodic updates mirror the changes in the country and at the same time look to the future. They also take into account research findings and theoretical positions about the nature of language; its use in reading, writing, and oral communication; and the factors that support or inhibit effective language use. And as electronic media have advanced, the statements have incorporated new concepts of language and language use. Although it would be difficult to document statistically, the pace of change in the profession clearly seems to have grown more rapid, as evidenced in the differences between the 1976 and 1986 statements and between the 1986 and 1996 editions. In the introduction to the 1986 *Guidelines,* Denny Wolfe, Chair of the NCTE Standing Committee on Teacher Preparation and Certification that prepared those guidelines, identified the changes that had taken place since the writing of the previous statement:

> This revision, like other such NCTE documents which precede it, acknowledges changes in educational theory, research, and practice that inevitably determine the emphases in preservice teacher education programs. Since the 1976 *Statement,* several factors have emerged or intensified—factors which must be considered in any document advancing recommendations for English language arts teacher education programs. Among these factors are the increased use of standardized testing for both students and teachers; the growing influence of psycholinguistics and sociolinguistics on the teaching of English

as a second language; pedagogy for exceptional students; recent developments in technology, especially the microcomputer and calls for "computer literacy"; a variety of learning theories in composition, accompanied by process-oriented approaches to the teaching of writing; influential literary theories developed since the "New Criticism"; research investigating connections between language and cognition; and the language-for-learning movement. (p. 1)

In the decade since those words were written, the movement into an electronic age has increased exponentially, so that computers now populate nearly every school and many classrooms. Students routinely compose, edit, and publish their essays, poems, and other creations on the computer. Clearly "computer literacy" is now an essential tool for success in most schools, and increasing numbers of colleges and universities require students to come equipped not just with computer skills but with their own computer hardware; and once students are on campus, they may find their residence hall rooms equipped with access to electronic mail and online services.

Another issue raised in the 1986 *Guidelines* was the criticism of American education that had appeared a few years earlier:

In the early 1980s, a spate of reports documented and analyzed the state of contemporary American public schooling, among them *High School: A Report on Secondary Education in America* (1983), *A Place Called School: Prospects for the Future* (1983), *A Nation at Risk: The Imperative for Educational Reform* (1983), and *Horace's Compromise: The Dilemma of the American High School* (1984). These and other reports called for radical reforms of public school curricula and of the preparation and professional advancement of teachers. (pp. 1–2)

Today, the criticism of American schools has become more frequent and more strident than that of ten years ago. Talk-show hosts, home-schoolers, politicians, and self-appointed experts regularly castigate the schools for failing to educate America's youth. Schools are condemned for producing illiterate graduates. Expertise in "correct" language use is declared lacking but sorely needed. Students are expected to write well and speak effectively, to think analytically and present ideas forcefully. Familiarity with the literature and culture of the Western world—if not the world in general—is proclaimed important because it creates "cultural literacy" and passes on the historic values of the culture.

Yet while critics are calling for reform in our schools, funding for education programs, including those that support the preparation of teachers, is cut. Ignoring this withdrawal of support, critics direct much of their blame at classroom teachers and at the ways in which teachers are prepared. Although not all teachers of the English language arts may agree with the reasoning of the critics, at least we can be sure that what we teach—and what and how we teach teachers to teach—is seen as important even by our most severe detractors.

Through recent and ongoing efforts to create standards for what students acquire through language arts education, the profession itself has become conscious of many areas of contention among teacher educators. However, as stated in the 1986 *Guidelines*,

[I]t is important for NCTE to affirm what it believes to be significant in the preparation of teachers of English language arts; at the same time, NCTE is obliged to suggest guidelines for others to follow in developing programs that prepare teachers of English language arts at all instructional levels. (p. 2)

Doing so is clearly no easy task. And, although essential, finding agreement within the profession becomes increasingly difficult. Today, as opinions about the roles of schools and teachers continue to multiply, those of us who teach the English language arts—a diverse body with strongly held views—disagree among ourselves about our own subject and our own view of the role of the teacher. For example, the strongest advocate of "cultural literacy" is himself an English professor; yet even some who disagree with his position have also raised serious questions about current school literature programs. Thus, as the Standing Committee worked its way through many meetings, drafts, e-mail conversations, revisions, and a barrage of computer disks, these differences within the profession, as well as those raging in the public arena, surfaced in our responses to each other. One member of the committee termed our efforts at finding the voice of the profession as "shooting at a moving target," and we all agreed.

PREPARING ENGLISH MAJORS AND PREPARING ENGLISH MAJORS WHO WILL BE TEACHERS

The committee began the development of these *Guidelines* by making a distinction between what a program for English majors should require as outcomes and what, in addition or differently, a program to prepare English language arts teachers should require. The distinction seemed a helpful one, and we held to it throughout our three years of work. We were careful to keep in mind that the distinction was not one of the programs' worth but one of differing purposes. We agreed that both programs, but especially the one for teachers, should produce individuals whose experiences have been such that they know that "all language processes are integrated and, hence, that language study should be approached holistically" (1986 *Guidelines*, p. 3).

The members of the committee, however, found themselves in at least partial disagreement concerning a belief that permeated both the 1976 and 1986 versions of the *Guidelines*:

> English is viewed not only as a body of knowledge but also as a process, an activity— something one does. That is, one uses and responds to language in a variety of ways and in a variety of contexts. Teaching English and language arts as process and activity, then, requires the building of student-centered, interactive classroom environments. (1986 *Guidelines*, p. 3)

Although we agreed on the importance of processes, we disagreed with the previous statements' focus on "student-centered, interactive" learning alone; we believe that direct teaching also has a place in the education of teachers of the English language arts. We do concur that teachers at all grade levels need to understand what language is, how it is acquired and developed, and how to provide students with experiences and opportunities to use their language in order to develop expertise in communication. And we agree with the earlier committees that diversity of situations is important, especially as students move into a world that is becoming more and more heterogeneous.

Although "process" has become a negative word in many people's lexicon, these guidelines reflect a perspective that recognizes that language use *is* a process: a process that begins with the use of oral language in very young children, and continues throughout life;

a process that is holistic (itself a controversial term) and integrates the traditional "language arts" of reading, writing, speaking, and listening. Research and theory in the field of linguistics from the last ten years have added support for this belief that undergirds both the 1986 and 1996 *Guidelines*. It has become increasingly clear that language development must be active rather than passive, whether a teacher is dealing with reading skills or literature, with oral or written composition.

WHAT SHOULD BEGINNING TEACHERS KNOW, BE ABLE TO DO, AND BELIEVE?

The current guidelines represent the committee's best view of what the profession might say about what teachers of the English language arts should believe, know, and be able to do in classrooms. We see them as building on the areas discussed in the 1976 *Statement* and the 1986 *Guidelines*. The members of the committee agreed early on that one's preparation to be a teacher does not end with graduation from a college or university. As stated in the introduction to the 1986 *Guidelines*:

> This document, like the 1976 *Statement* and earlier NCTE recommendations, takes for granted that the education of teachers of English language arts is a continuing, lifelong process. No prospective English language arts teacher can attain, through an undergraduate teacher education program or even a program leading to permanent certification, a total command of the art and science of teaching; therefore, teachers should not consider their preparation ended when they receive permanent certificates and tenure in their jobs. Teaching involves the growth of an individual as a professional, as a scholar, and as a human being—growth which develops only through experience in teaching and through lifelong learning. (p. 4)

So we considered carefully what was different about preparing a beginning teacher and what was needed for the lifelong education of teachers. We agreed with what the 1986 Standing Committee stated:

> The preservice teacher education program should initiate and develop certain knowledge, pedagogical abilities, and attitudes which will be the foundation for the teacher's subsequent professional career—for the English language arts teacher as scholar, decision-maker, and agent of curriculum change. Consequently, the present document advances recommendations for the essential elements of a preservice education program. (p. 4)

Our guidelines, then, state what English language arts teachers should believe, know, and be able to do as teachers. They also lay out a set of initial dispositions, knowledge, and pedagogical knowledge and skills for the beginning teacher, and they set goals for the career teacher. Teacher education programs should ensure that their graduates are knowledgeable, thoughtful, and skillful at the beginning of their careers, and that they have the potential to become models of effective teaching. The guidelines do not try to set levels of attainment for each attitude, each type of knowledge, each set of skills. They assume that teacher education programs, and the professionals who act in them, will be able to set reasonable levels of achievement for the beginners and help classroom practitioners to set reasonable goals for themselves.

As has been true in earlier versions of the *Guidelines*, the committee has not attempted to establish an English language arts teacher-education *program* with a predetermined set of courses or other experiences. Nor do the guidelines deal with questions of undergraduate and graduate preparation. Rather, the committee has identified the outcomes that any program designed to prepare English language arts teachers should produce, recognizing that there are many alternative ways for programs to reach those outcomes. At the same time, the committee looked at several model programs and attempted to determine what they have in common. These broad elements, while basic to successful programs, are descriptive and not prescriptive (see the chapter "Characteristics of Effective Teacher-Preparation Programs for English Language Arts").

The use of the term "English language arts" throughout has been intentional in this document, as it was in the 1986 version, and the term refers to teaching at both the elementary and secondary school levels. Sometimes distinctions are made between elementary and secondary preservice education, because of the unique responsibilities, demands, and circumstances of each educational level. But the essential elements of effective teacher-preparation programs apply to both elementary and secondary teachers of English language arts.

USING THESE *GUIDELINES*

This document is divided into a number of sections. First, it delineates a set of basic principles (diversity, content knowledge, pedagogical knowledge and skills, opportunity, and dynamic literacy) which underlie the entire document. The next three chapters detail the attitudes, knowledge, and pedagogical skills and knowledge that teachers of the English language arts should possess. Those chapters, which are the heart of the guidelines, are followed by chapters designed to help the reader place the attitudes, knowledge, and pedagogy sections in a meaningful context. Because the committee recognized that attitudes cannot be separated fully from knowledge or pedagogy, just as those areas cannot be separated from the others, we have included a table that shows the interrelations among those elements. In addition, since national standards for the English language arts were nearing completion at the same time as this document, the committee prepared a discussion of the relationship of the *Guidelines* to national standards.

In order to show what elements are found in effective teacher-education programs, the committee has included a set of brief models and a discussion of their common features. Since we see preservice teacher preparation as only the beginning of the process, the committee has added two documents earlier prepared by commissions of the Conference on English Education—one dealing with the vital issue of effective transition to teaching and the other presenting a set of principles for effective inservice programs. Additionally, we share a personal narrative about the needs of a beginning teacher: Larry Crapse (in the Appendix) draws on his experience and offers insights into making the first year of teaching a success.

In the closing chapter of the *Guidelines,* we identify some of the unresolved issues related to preparation programs for English teachers. There are many differing views within the profession about the nature of successful teaching and learning, and we hope this chapter will help guide the discussions that must take place as we seek agreement on these issues.

While *Guidelines for the Preparation of Teachers of English Language Arts* is, of course, not the final word on teacher-education programs, it can be a vehicle to focus thought and discussion on the vital task of preparing English language arts teachers. Teacher educators at colleges and universities are one audience for this document. Another consists of practicing teachers of the English language arts, who themselves are important teacher educators because of their roles as models, supervisors, and mentors. We hope that the *Guidelines* will provoke a debate which includes both of these groups of teacher educators, as well as administrators, school board members, and other citizens concerned about the success of students in our schools.

Statement of Underlying Principles

As members of the Standing Committee on Teacher Preparation and Certification developed these guidelines, we identified a set of principles which underlay the more detailed and specific items of the three organizing areas of attitudes, knowledge, and pedagogy. These general principles govern the detailed beliefs, understandings, and skills that we believe must mark the teacher who emerges from an effective English language arts teacher-preparation program.

PRINCIPLES OF DIVERSITY

English language arts education programs should provide teachers with the attitudes, content, and pedagogical knowledge and skills so that they will:

1. Recognize and value the diversity of students.
2. Promote communication among cultures to foster mutual understanding.
3. Draw upon the diversity of students to enrich and enhance their academic achievement.
4. Enable students to construct meaning from multiple sources.
5. Encourage the development of students' multiple ways of knowing and understanding.

PRINCIPLES OF CONTENT KNOWLEDGE

English language arts education programs should provide teachers with content knowledge so that they will:

1. Understand the role that literature plays in the development and understanding of human cultures.
2. Understand that composing is a practice that covers a wide range of processes, functions, purposes, rhetorical situations, and categories of discourse.
3. Display a broad view of what constitutes texts, including both print and nonprint media), and demonstrate an understanding that technological advancements can change both what is considered as text and how text is prepared.
4. Know and be able to use and teach a wide range of critical and interpretive approaches to literature.
5. Know and understand that the uses of language and literature vary among cultures.
6. Know and understand that the various rapidly developing uses of media and technology are becoming integral to teaching practice.
7. Understand the nature of the English language in all its dimensions and recognize and respect the varieties of that language.
8. Value languages native to students and their families.

PRINCIPLES OF PEDAGOGICAL KNOWLEDGE AND SKILL

English language arts education programs should provide teachers with pedagogical knowledge and skill so that they will:

1. Understand and be skillful in planning and implementing instruction that recognizes students' interests, abilities, and modes of learning.
2. Understand and be skillful in employing authentic ways of assessing students' learning.
3. Understand that there are multiple positions or orientations for teaching English language arts and that many of these are valid in certain contexts and in relation to students' needs and backgrounds.

PRINCIPLES OF OPPORTUNITY

English language arts education programs should provide teachers with opportunities to:

1. Develop teaching/learning processes through experiences with a wide range of verbal, visual, technological, and creative media.

2. Expand themselves as literate individuals who use their critical, intellectual, and aesthetic abilities to participate in a democratic society.

3. Experience a wide range of literature consistent with their own and their students' motivations, interests, and intellects.

4. Participate in model classrooms that function as communities of learners and users of language.

5. Experience and consider the uses of multiple means of assessment.

6. Develop the sense of a professional community and a desire for professional growth that comes with being an English teacher.

7. Reflect on their own and other's instruction as a means for self-improvement and self-understanding.

PRINCIPLES OF DYNAMIC LITERACY

English language arts teacher preparation programs should recruit, nurture, and graduate new teachers who:

1. Write with proficiency and pleasure, read widely for enlightenment and growth, and participate in cultural events in their school and in the wider community.

2. Write about and share their experiences as writers and as readers with their students.

Attitudes of Effective
English Language Arts Teachers

In any profession, there are certain sets of attitudes essential to the effective conduct of that profession. For English language arts teachers, these integral attitudes include: valuing all forms of human communication, including oral, written, pictorial, and signed; valuing the traditions, culture, and language experiences of learners; valuing the responsibility to assist students in learning about many forms and uses of language; valuing the innate power, right, and responsibility of learners to shape their own education; valuing the role of literature, both as an art form and as a means of understanding the human experience; valuing composing—written, oral, and visual—as a means of discovering self, learning about the world, creating meaning, and sharing with others; valuing technology as a potential means for understanding self and as a tool for teaching and learning; valuing professional growth; valuing personal experience and communication as bases for growth and as ways to obtain new knowledge and understanding; and valuing both the products and the process of re-search.

A positive professional self-image is a cornerstone for enhancing the learning environment. English language arts teachers should respect their own uniqueness as individuals and as teachers and the richness they bring to their classrooms. They must be committed to professional growth, and they must realize that, as they expand their horizons, they increase their ability to serve their students. They should draw upon a variety of materials to help students explore conditions and concerns that are the focus of the curriculum. They should see that their students are actively engaged in problem solving and decision making that may not lead to one correct answer, and they should respect the ambiguity of an expectation, position, or role. Thus, teachers of English language arts need to develop the following attitudes:

1. A recognition that all students can learn and are worthy of a teacher's attention in the English language arts classroom.

Research suggests a high correlation between student performance and teacher expectation. Students sometimes receive differing responses from teachers based on such factors as standardized test data, past classroom performance, race, physical qualities, and gender. Teachers should be sensitive to student needs so that all students, regardless of differences, receive encouragement, support, and opportunities to learn.

2. A desire to use the English language arts curriculum to help students become familiar with diverse peoples and cultures.

In a multicultural society, teachers must help students achieve cross-cultural understanding and appreciation. Teachers must be willing to seek and to use materials which represent linguistic and artistic achievements from a variety of ethnic and cultural perspectives. In such diverse cultural contexts, students explore their own perceptions and values.

3. A respect and enthusiasm for the individual language, dialect, bi-dialectal competence, and other language variations of each student.

Teachers must treat respectfully the language and dialect that each student brings into the classroom, recognizing that every dialect has an appropriate use. While providing students access to standard oral and written forms of English, teachers should establish an environment that encourages respect, enthusiasm, and appreciation for all forms of language.

4. A conviction that teachers help students grow by encouraging creative and appropriate uses of language.

Growth in language facility occurs when students experiment with language and receive respectful and appropriately critical response from teachers and peers. Teachers must build classroom environments characterized by both freedom and discipline. In such classrooms, students take risks by shaping complex ideas through language (both oral and written), and they learn to accept responses and criticism that help them improve their language abilities.

5. A willingness to seek a match between students' needs and teachers' objectives, methods, and materials for instruction in English language arts that places students' needs at the center of the curriculum.

Teachers must be able to prepare objectives, select instructional methods, and use materials for groups of learners, while also tailoring instruction to students' individual needs and learning styles. Teachers must be able to articulate to administrators, supervisors, and parents the rationales for their approaches to instruction.

6. A willingness to encourage students to respond critically to different media and communications technology.

Teachers must make instructional use of students' exposure to and interest in communications technology and popular media. They must be willing to use nonprint media—for example, television and film—as well as print, laser discs, and interactive media to help students grow both in the use of language and in understanding human behavior. To facilitate such growth, teachers should encourage divergent responses to the forms and content of technology and media.

7. A commitment to continued professional growth in the teaching of the English language arts.

Teachers must acquire a sense of belonging to their professional community. They must both contribute to it and be nurtured by it; therefore, they must be active participants in local, state, and national organizations that promote professional development. In addition, they must develop a commitment to lifelong learning of the content and methodology of their discipline.

8. A pride in teaching the English language arts and a willingness to take informed stands on issues of professional concern.

Caring about what one does is essential to success and self-esteem. Teachers who recognize the importance of their work are intensely aware of pedagogical and sociopolitical issues that affect them and their students. As a consequence, they promote helpful changes and resist those they see as harmful.

9. A sensitivity to the impact that events and developments in the world outside the school have on teachers, their colleagues, their students, and the English language arts curriculum.

The English language arts curriculum must consider forces that influence human values and daily life. Such connections between school and the outside world help sustain students' motivation to learn. Therefore, teachers must be attuned to both the immediate and long-term effects of social issues and world events. This sensitivity enables them to link current issues and events with the goals of English language arts instruction.

10. An enthusiasm for developing lifelong habits of mind to facilitate clear thinking and critical judgment.

Teachers of the English language arts should employ instruction techniques that foster and nurture the cognitive and metacognitive processes required for clear thinking and critical judgment. The educational experiences that teachers provide should enable students to view their environments and the world in general from a problem-solving perspective and to draw conclusions from a wide variety of sources. In addition, students should acquire from such instruction a positive attitude about such analysis and decision making. A process of inquiry that promotes reflective thought and concern is a hallmark of a vigorous, collaborative learning community. Because much learning takes place beyond school walls, teachers must be aware of and concerned about the actions and efforts of their students in those larger contexts.

11. A recognition of the value of diversity of opinion.

Respect for the points of view and opinions of others is critical to mental, emotional, and intellectual growth. Teachers must, therefore, provide students with opportunities for and guidance in expressing themselves orally and in writing. They should expose students to various and differing opinions on topics taken from literature, speech, and media presentations. In addition, they should encourage students to express their reactions frankly in order to develop their listening skills and their willingness to consider ideas that differ from their own.

12. A desire to promote the arts and humanities in the daily lives of all students.

Teachers of the English language arts must seek ways to integrate elements of the arts and the humanities in their daily instruction in order to create a balanced academic experience for their students. By incorporating traditional and current music, art, philosophy, etc., in the students' academic lives, teachers support an understanding that such aspects of human culture are important for the individual student and for the health of the community.

13. A commitment to encourage students to read and write about the special insights and feelings they derive from literature.

Literature provides students with opportunities to make use of their own lives and feelings to create fresh works that explain those lives and feelings. Teachers must not only value such creations but also provide opportunities for students to express their creativity and to share the results with other students, parents, and other adults. From such positive experiences, students develop an enthusiasm for reading and learn to share their responses with others.

Content Knowledge for Effective English Language Arts Teachers

In English language arts teacher-preparation programs, the curricula must include not only that knowledge of literature, language, and the process of composing suitable for majors in English, but also the specialized knowledge appropriate for teachers of the subject. The preparation of teachers must include knowledge of and practice in the use of those instructional methods that research and best practice show as effective in promoting learning. Thus, this section of the *Guidelines* assumes that "knowledge base" means *more* than the basic knowledge of content-specific English language arts; it also refers to an understanding of that basic content knowledge in the *context* in which it will be used—the English language arts classroom.

The knowledge base of effective English language arts teachers can be divided into nine general areas: language development, language analysis, language composition, written discourse, reading and literature, media, instructional media, assessment, and research and theory.

LANGUAGE DEVELOPMENT

1. Growth in language is a developmental process.

English language arts teachers need a comprehensive understanding of developmental theories and processes by which people acquire, understand, and use language. This understanding is necessary so that teachers can help strengthen students' language abilities throughout their schooling. Students enhance these abilities by using and processing language in various contexts. Teachers need to know the relationship of language development to the fundamental principles and characteristics of human growth so that they set their expectations of a student's language use and development according to student readiness and achievement levels. By providing developmentally appropriate experiences, teachers can reduce learning anxiety and help students become linguistically mature.

2. There is a close relationship between how home language, native language, dialect, and a second language are acquired and developed.

Initial language acquisition occurs in the home and in a second-language environment as the need to decipher or to communicate arises. Different from initial acquisition, language development is a natural process that children begin as they expand and monitor their personal language based on what they hear, understand, and use. English language arts teachers need to be aware of the ways in which language is acquired and developed so they can provide situations where students can appropriately develop their language skills.

3. Speaking, listening, writing, reading, observing, and thinking are interrelated.

Language development occurs as students use all the language processes and understand the relationships among them. Oral language is a fundamental means of learning, and it serves as the basis for learning reading and writing skills. Research also indicates close relationships between language and thought development. Awareness of these principles and of the holistic nature of language and thinking equips teachers at all levels not only to use integrated approaches in teaching the language arts but also to provide instruction that focuses on each aspect of language.

4. Social, cultural, and economic environments are intrinsic parts of language learning.

Students learn language through use, their need to know, and their environments; in turn, they need to learn to respond to, respect, and understand the communication of others. Teachers need to understand language variation so they can help students recognize and use language appropriate to different occasions. Therefore, teachers need to know how to acquire knowledge and understanding of the social and cultural environments of the communities from which their students come. In addition, to be effective, teachers must be able to provide opportunities for students to practice language beyond the academic environment of the classroom.

LANGUAGE ANALYSIS

5. The English language is dynamic rather than static.

Teachers must be prepared to help students see English as a language which has undergone and is still undergoing many changes which keep it vital and rich in meaning. Studies of major developments in the history of language may help students cultivate an interest in and remain fascinated with the language. Therefore, teachers need to know the major periods of language history and the significant changes in language associated with those periods. Further, teachers need to be aware of continuing change in language and how change is evidenced in contemporary language use.

6. There are many versions of English.

Because of their diverse backgrounds, students may bring many language patterns to the classroom. Teachers need to understand the nature and sources of language variety and to develop a global perspective on English. By understanding the major semantic, syntactical, and auditory systems of English, teachers will be able to provide ways to discuss language and its production with students and, therefore, to help students understand how languages function. Teachers should understand the significance of grammar systems as one way to discuss language, and they should understand the relationship of scholarly grammar systems to the production of language. This emphasis in instruction, however, should be based on the use of language rather than on an abstract study of it. Teachers need to provide opportunities for students to use nonacademic as well as academic English. In doing so, they can help students understand when to use formal structures and when informal structures are appropriate. Teachers also must understand that the meaning and function of grammars are grounded in language, rather than thinking that grammar systems drive language.

LANGUAGE COMPOSITION

7. There are processes and elements in the act of composing that are crucial to oral, visual, and written discourse.

Rich oral language experiences are closely related to writing performance. Although both speaking and writing usually take place in a social context, oral text is sometimes thought of as informal and as often preceding written discourse. In truth, both oral and written discourse contain like elements and follow processes that teachers need to understand in order to help students develop and extend communication skills. Technology has enlarged these processes to include visual discourse through the use of digital media as well as through such traditional media as film, video, photographs, and pictures. Visual discourse, then, is closely linked with oral and written discourse. While constructing meaning from their own visual experience and that of others, students compose and evaluate visual representations. Teachers need to recognize that these representations vary from culture to culture.

Furthermore, all teachers must know that much practice with expressive language is necessary for the development of voice or style in all forms of discourse. Such practice requires speaking and writing for various purposes in a wide variety of forms for many different audiences.

Teachers also must be aware of equity issues in language, such as the extension of language codes and registers beyond the limits of standard or formal English; the nature and use of academic discourse and other forms of writing and speaking to expand rather than inhibit student expression; and the use and, therefore, validation of global forms of English in classroom conversation.

Teachers need to provide environments where "public literacy" practice may take place: where students learn how to take part in public discussions whether written or oral, where they participate in deciding issues and know how to find information which enables them to take part. Teachers need to know that there are "drafts" in the oral and visual as well as the written composing process. They need to understand the many models and theories of the writing process, because this knowledge will enable them to choose approaches that meet their instructional needs. They also need to be aware of the usefulness of techniques to improve oral and written discourse, such as self- and peer assessment, as well as teacher assessment.

8. Language and visual images influence thinking and actions.

Verbal and visual languages are powerful influences upon human thinking and behavior. By examining relationships between verbal and visual languages, teachers can help students understand how to distinguish among the purposes of language and how users of language achieve these purposes. Teachers also need to be able to help students recognize differences in visual images as well as in written and oral language—for example, between fact and opinion, between symbol and text, between truth and propaganda.

WRITTEN DISCOURSE

9. Writing is a form of inquiry, reflection, and expression.

Writing is a major form of inquiry which enables students to act effectively in their immediate social environment and in the larger world. Thus, teachers must understand how language enhances and refines such inquiry. For this, they must have knowledge of writing as a process and as a product, and they must be aware of the impact of technology on student writing.

Teachers who learn about and continuously practice various aspects of composing—prewriting, drafting, revising, editing, publishing, evaluating—are better able to teach those processes well to their students. Therefore, teachers must practice their own writing skills in a variety of forms.

READING AND LITERATURE

10. Readers respond to and interpret what they read in a constructive or transactional process.

Teachers must understand how students respond personally to works of literature and how these personal responses create their interpretations of those works. Teachers need to give students the freedom to deal with their own reactions to texts, creating environments for conversations about and with texts through speech, writing, and other forms. Students need to understand and value ways of responding to literature, such as identifying with texts, conceptualizing, visualizing, and reflecting on their own experiences. To foster students' personal responses to literature, teachers need to be aware of differing interpretative stances or approaches and to assist students in selecting such stances or approaches. Teachers must also provide an environment that allows students to develop critical insights and that supports them in identifying their favorite pieces of literature.

11. Proficient readers consciously create and discover meaning and monitor their own comprehension.

Understanding how people read enables English language arts teachers at every level to identify students' ease or difficulties in comprehending printed material. Theories and research suggest that (1) reading is a constructive process in which readers use structures of previous knowledge and experience to make meaning from print; (2) readers tend to respond in similar ways as well as in singular ways; and (3) meanings and responses are sustained by readers' awareness of how satisfactorily they comprehend what they read. Teachers must know how a text operates, how it shapes thought, and how it manipulates emotion. With such understanding, they can use questions and comments to encourage students to analyze their responses and the causes of those responses.

12. There is an extensive body of literature and literary genres in English and in translation—including the well-known and the little-known, the commonly used in the curriculum and the rarely used, the traditional and the unusual—representing a worldview appropriate for the classroom.

Literature that captures the imagination of children and adolescents is as diverse as youth. Consequently, English language arts teachers at all levels need broad and deep experiences with literature. They need to engage in oral and written conversations about a variety of texts as well as interact with the texts themselves. They should read on several levels, including but not limited to reading directly for information, understanding, and pleasure.

Teachers need to be able to guide students to become independent readers by providing them with appropriate choices and by encouraging self-monitoring of reading habits and processes; they must be familiar with a rich and varied store of literature that will engage their students. In addition to using literature in anthologies and other school texts, teachers need to know how to find other literature sources. They need to use contemporary children's and young adult literature, and other appropriate literature written specifically for the age and interest levels of their students. Likewise, in order to expand their students' experiences with literature, teachers must themselves be knowledgeable about literature by male and female writers, by and about people of many racial, ethnic, and cultural groups, and by authors from many countries and cultures in all parts of the world. In addition, teachers need to understand that their students have stories to share from their own lives as well as from their reading.

13. Literature is a source for exploring and interpreting the experiences of human beings—their achievements, frustrations, foibles, values, and conflicts.

Teachers of the English language arts must see literature as the core, the humane center, of the English curriculum. They must be aware of the unique opportunities literature provides for understanding human experience: as the 1983 NCTE brochure, *Essentials of English,* put it, through literature "students broaden their insights, allowing them to experience vicariously places, people, and events otherwise unavailable to them, adding delight and wonder to their daily lives."

Literature affirms our common humanity, illuminates our differences, and documents how different people at different times have perceived and approached an infinite variety of human problems and aspirations. To help students understand how literature celebrates humanity, teachers must develop effective ways to allow students to talk and write about varied forms of literature. They need to model good reading habits for students, showing that reading can be done for pleasure as well as for academic purposes.

MEDIA

14. Knowledge of the power and the potential of print and nonprint media is necessary to understanding contemporary culture.

Teachers need to be familiar with print and nonprint media and understand how people are influenced by them. They must provide students with the means to appraise the messages they find both in and out of the classroom. Teachers also need to understand how nonprint media act as texts as well as visual symbols, and they should encourage students to construct meaning from these texts and not see them as transmitted reality. It is important that teachers themselves be able to identify the ways in which messages are communicated in the media and to be able to judge these messages—that is, for example, to separate fact from opinion, logic from fallacy.

Teachers must be able to prepare students to understand the range of media—for example, print and electronic news, television, advertisements, music, videos, games—and their effects on individuals and groups. By understanding both the negative and positive influences of various media, teachers can assist their students in recognizing and dealing with those influences. Teachers must help their students be aware of the immediacy of various media and the power their messages have. Verbal and visual media are found throughout daily living, and new technologies continue to extend modes of communicating ideas and learning about the ideas of others. Therefore, teachers should be conversant with new technologies, especially those which may have an impact on their classrooms and students.

INSTRUCTIONAL MEDIA

15. Instructional technology can aid, as well as add to, the English language arts curriculum.

Instructional technology has changed the way classrooms look and the way students learn. English language arts teachers need to recognize the potential of media as teaching vehicles. They need to be able to use multiple resources such as visual materials, technological devices, interactive tools, and artifacts of contemporary culture. These can provide fresh access to the English language arts curriculum and support more efficient and productive learning. English language arts teachers need to be cognizant of the range of television, film, magazines, course software, newspapers, and other materials that are available and of interest to students. Of equal importance for teachers is the ability to discriminate between valuable instructional media and those that are useless or that potentially run counter to the objectives of their curricula.

ASSESSMENT

16. Student learning should be described through the use of a variety of assessments.

Given the complex and personal nature of language, no single test or other measure can give a comprehensive and accurate picture of what a student has learned. Teachers must understand the strengths and limitations of specific assessment instruments and techniques. They need to construct and provide models by practicing these assessment techniques with their own learning and be able to select the appropriate assessment vehicles for a particular classroom level or curricular objective. Teachers must realize that they cannot rely on one type or one assessment procedure to determine mastery of content or skill. They also need to understand that qualitative measures such as observation and interview are as appropriate as quantitative measures such as tests.

Teachers, therefore, must be familiar with authentic assessment techniques and procedures, such as reflective writing, student- and teacher-developed guidelines or checklists, learning records, portfolio presentations, and exhibitions. They need to know several ways of assessing student writing performance, such as holistic, primary trait, and analytic scoring of writing. They should be familiar with a range of systems, such as learning records, that describe student progress in all language processes. Teachers also need to assess student achievements and needs using formal and informal methods, including observing students at work, keeping anecdotal records, and recording their interpretation of these observations. They also should use individual and small-group conferencing as interim and final assessment tools.

17. Standardized testing that alone attempts to describe students according to specific scores does not adequately reflect or support students' learning potential.

Teachers need to be aware that data from standardized measures are limited as determiners of growth in English language arts. They should understand the negative impact that such testing measures can have, if misused, on curriculum and instruction. They should understand the problems associated with relying on any one type of testing instrument or procedure to determine student learning potential. Teachers, therefore, need to be able to determine the appropriate formal and informal ways to evaluate student growth in the English language arts.

RESEARCH AND THEORY

18. Knowledge of major research findings and theory in the content of the discipline and in issues and trends that affect curriculum is essential for creating a productive teaching and learning environment.

English language arts teachers must know the major sources—for example, books, periodicals, reports, and proceedings—of research, theory, and the issues and trends that influence the content and pedagogy of their discipline. Teachers need to know how to take advantage of opportunities and resources, including electronic databases, to stay abreast of current research and theory in the English language arts and allied content pedagogy. Additionally, English language arts teachers need to understand and be able to use teacher-researcher models of classroom inquiry appropriately.

Pedagogical Knowledge and Skills Demonstrated by Effective English Language Arts Teachers

Because learning forms the mind rather than furnishes it, students come to the classroom not with empty minds waiting to be filled, but rather with minds already occupied with both previous experiences and present concerns. It is, however, in the *learning process* that students synthesize new experiences into what has been previously understood and thus reshape their understandings of the world in which they live. Meaning, therefore, is constructed when new experiences transform what learners already know; and sense of meaning comes through personal engagement and interpretation and through dialogue with others.

This view of learning requires teaching practices that help learners internalize, reshape, and transform new information rather than simply repeat newly presented information. It also requires students to generate, demonstrate, and exhibit their transformed understandings. In a learning process of this nature, attention is focused on the learner; this focus changes the role of the teacher and the nature of the learning environment. This perspective suggests that language is learned in operation. Students, therefore, must be surrounded by and engaged in talk, writing, and literature. By creating a learning community in which students work both independently and collaboratively, sharing their ideas, their experiences, and their ways of thinking, teachers enable students to become immersed in language in operation. Engaging learners in language, then, is the foundation for classroom activities.

The learning environment teachers create is closely allied to the professional development they have experienced. If they understand that students construct their own meaning from the world around them, teachers will design classrooms in which students will be engaged personally and socially in activities centered on them. The class will recognize that such activities are valuable, and both teacher and students will seek out opportunities for personal interpretation and group communication, conjecture, argument, and problem solving. Students and the teacher will value both independent and collaborative thinking; students' questions will be encouraged and explored, and validation of ideas will be expected. The learning environment is the key element in skillful teaching, for the dimensions of productive learning and teaching are embedded in that environment.

Therefore, teachers of the English language arts must understand and be proficient in the following areas: instructional planning; instructional performance; instructional assessment; instruction in oral, written, and visual languages; and instruction in reading, literature, and nonprint media.

INSTRUCTIONAL PLANNING

1. Structure English language arts holistically.

Because the English language arts curriculum is multidimensional and involves substance (literature, language, rhetoric), skills (reading, writing, viewing, listening, speaking), and processes (affective, cognitive, creative), the interconnectedness of these dimensions must be reflected when teachers select, design, and organize objectives, strategies, and materials. Organizational patterns such as themes, topics, and life experiences, as well as genres and similar types of approaches, will promote holistic structure. Given the public nature of education, teachers need to understand how state and locally established objectives, strategies, and materials can be incorporated into lessons and units that reflect such interconnectedness.

2. Structure the classroom in a manner that encourages students to work independently and collaboratively.

Knowledge created in discourse requires individuals to construct meaning and to engage in thinking with others. Students, therefore, need opportunities to work as individuals and in small groups or as a class. When carrying out a project of personal interest, students may need to work alone; when working to maximize their own and each other's learning, a small-group or whole-class organization may be best. Regardless of the structural pattern, however, active learning—in which students question their own and other students' ideas, and in which they explain and support those ideas—is an important aspect of overall learning.

3. Use a variety of materials and media.

Teachers need to use a rich variety of print and nonprint materials rather than relying on a single textbook. Resources include magazines, public radio and television, recorded music, paintings and sculptures, films and videos, as well as novels, nonfiction, poems, short stories, and plays. Teachers should include works in which ethnic groups and people of color are represented, works from around the globe, works from popular or contemporary culture, and works that allow for various levels of language skill. Teachers should also look to students' own suggestions as an important source of materials.

4. Plan interdisciplinary units.

Instruction that calls for subject matter across subject lines is increasingly seen by the profession as important, both because the integrated curriculum will increase richness and because it will give greater meaning to each of the disciplines. Teachers must understand the connection of English language arts to other disciplines and be able to plan interdisciplinary units with other teachers. Organizing an interdisciplinary unit is a cooperative endeavor; teachers must know the roles and responsibilities of teams and their members, how class time may be structured, how students are assigned to groups, and how common planning time is best used.

INSTRUCTIONAL PERFORMANCE

5. Create learning environments which promote respect for and understanding of individual academic, ethnic, racial, language, cultural, and gender differences.

Because meaning constructed by individuals is influenced by all facets of the individual's prior experiences, teachers need to apply their knowledge of students' language, cultural backgrounds, and cognitive characteristics to what they teach and how they teach it. A single strategy for teaching language and literature limits—possibly even excludes—students' involvement, and may hamper their eventual success. Teachers need to provide opportunities in which the central themes of English language arts subject matter are considered from as many cultural and intellectual viewpoints as possible. Differences in learning styles may mean some students prefer working in groups, sharing, and helping, while others prefer to work alone. Therefore, teachers must create learning environments that combine opportunities for students to work in groups or individually.

6. Stimulate students in an active, mind-engaging process.

An active, mind-engaging process is one in which students create, discover, and make sense of the English language arts. In a collaborative learning community, individual work is not only created but also shared with many audiences. Many voices are heard, enhancing the learner's ability to speak, write, read, view, and listen. The teacher makes possible a sharing of students' thoughts and ideas, the reactions of others to those thoughts and ideas, and each student's rethinking based on those reactions. Through such sharing, students discover alternatives that bring greater meaning to what they study. As they construct knowledge through shared experiences, they gain insights into not only the central themes of the English language arts but also the ways in which they learn.

7. Use student creations as a part of the instructional program.

Teachers should view student creations such as poems, essays, videos, songs, and visual illustrations as materials valuable for instruction and worthy of recognition by students, teachers, parents, and the community in general. Students need to see their products not merely as school exercises but as praiseworthy creations.

8. Incorporate technology.

Teachers must be knowledgeable about new developments in technology as well as proficient in applications of technologies already in classroom use, such as overhead projectors, VCRs, CD-ROMs, and word processors. Teachers must be skillful enough to assist students in using the technologies that enhance learning.

Teachers also need to be able to evaluate and determine appropriate uses of instructional technology and its products. They should be able to recognize when technology enhances learning and when it is counterproductive, and they should be able to judge the quality and worth of materials such as computer software, videos, and commercial transparencies.

INSTRUCTIONAL ASSESSMENT

9. Promote classroom discourse in which student thinking is respected and challenged by the teacher and other students.

Although the teacher plays a central role in promoting and assessing classroom discourse, each student's reflections can create new understandings. Clarification, justification of ideas, and framing of questions that provoke students' thinking all promote classroom discourse and serve as evaluations of it. To facilitate discourse, the teacher must be skillful in helping students make connections among aspects of content and the learners' experiences, reading, ideas, and problems. The teacher also needs to be adept at helping students serve as the audience for one another's discourse.

10. Use frequent and immediate feedback to help students construct new understandings and acquire new skills.

To effectively evaluate student performance, teachers must be able to integrate various forms of assessment into the everyday learning experiences of students. One way to do this is for teachers to offer frequent and immediate feedback; used well, this approach engages students as well as the teacher in the assessment process on an almost daily basis. Involving students in the assessment of their own performance also creates opportunities for them to take risks, to try out innovative ideas, and to exhibit what they have internalized and learned through application.

Assessment should include both process and product measures. Teachers need to be skillful at noting each student's activity at each stage of the learning process, as well as at judging the quality of any finished product.

11. Develop ways to communicate assessment methods and results to different audiences.

Teachers must be able to select, create, and use testing methods appropriate to their instructional practices and their students; establish valid grading systems; and communicate a realistic picture of student progress. They must be able to articulate to students, parents, administrators, and other community members the standards of achievement established for the class, how achievement is measured, and the progress being made by individual students. Teachers must keep in mind that some instructional practices—such as whole language approaches to literacy, integrating the curriculum, and thematic teaching— are more process-oriented and require forms of assessment different from those used for more traditional ways of teaching. Such assessment tools and processes may be new to students and parents and may need additional explanation.

12. Use assessment outcomes to improve instruction.

Teachers should use the information gathered through assessment to improve instruction. They should make context-based decisions, taking into account a particular classroom, with a particular group of students from a range of family and cultural backgrounds. When learning experiences are integrated with various forms of assessment, that assessment provides practical knowledge; reflection on such knowledge can become the basis for selecting alternative learning strategies, forms of testing, grading systems, room arrangement, and for making other changes to improve instruction.

INSTRUCTION IN ORAL, WRITTEN, AND VISUAL LANGUAGES

13. Enrich and expand the learner's language resources for different social and cultural settings.

Teachers should provide opportunities for students to practice various language patterns. Activities can be planned that will help students assess the different situations they find themselves in and help them employ the English usage required by those situations. At the same time, teachers need to be able to strengthen students' pride and respect for the varieties of English that they and others in their communities use. Teachers must know how to use language variations as a resource to expand students' use and appreciation of language.

14. Engage learners in discussion, interpretation, and evaluation of ideas, whether presented in oral, written, or visual form.

Language usage is learned best in purposeful efforts to communicate ideas, facts, feelings, and values. Teachers need to actively involve their students in varied experiences with oral, written, and visual language. They need to use real-life activities such as classroom demonstrations, visual imagery of certain experiences, metaphor, and drama. Such activities should focus on the meaning of everyday experiences and offer students genuine opportunities to communicate.

15. Design instruction that reflects language as a human creation.

In the exploration of language, learners must realize that the invention of language is an ongoing process of which they are a part. Teachers need to be able to design instruction that will help students appreciate that language is a dynamic, constantly evolving creation, uniquely diverse with a rich history. They must be skillful in providing opportunities for students to consider their language in different real-world contexts and to understand that they can draw on their past experiences with language or create new language possibilities. The important key is to help learners see the direct connection of language study to their own lives and interests.

INSTRUCTION IN READING, LITERATURE, AND NONPRINT MEDIA

16. Build a reading, listening, and viewing community where students respond, interpret, think critically, and contrast ideas with others.

So that reading becomes an interactive process, teachers must be skillful in asking open-ended questions rather than questions with predetermined answers. They must also be effective in designing activities that challenge students to step outside themselves and view situations from the perspectives of others. For example, students might be asked to consider how a piece of fiction or a dramatic work might be different were it presented from the viewpoint of someone other than the main character. This type of activity allows students to share their initial responses and understandings and move toward increasingly complex comprehension.

17. Engage learners in transactions with literature.

In the literary experience, both the reader and the text play important roles in the meaning-making process. Literary texts are sources of intellectual, emotional, and aesthetic experiences from which individual readers create meaning. Teachers must be skillful in stimulating transactions with literature through instructional devices such as response journals, in-class explorations of texts, consideration of similarities and differences in student responses, and reflection on and analysis of student responses. From such transactions with many types of literature, students can learn to distinguish among literary genres and styles, perceive thematic patterns, and understand the importance of historical contexts for literature.

18. Promote media literacy.

Teachers must be able to guide students in preparing nonprint materials, such as storyboards or sound recordings, and in preparing and creating multimedia presentations. Students need to construct meaning through different media, analyze their transactions with media texts, and create their own media texts and performances. Teachers must help students to explore contemporary media as extensions of literature and as entities in and of themselves. They need to understand and to be skillful in teaching the possibilities and limitations of media texts, such as film, video, and television.

Interrelations:
Attitudes, Knowledge, and Pedagogy

The teaching of the English language arts is a holistic, dynamic, and constructive process. English language arts teachers are as diverse as the students and the language they teach, yet they are called upon to create learning environments and experiences that bring students and language together in a shared community. This implies an inextricable interconnectedness among the three strands of teacher preparation: attitudes, knowledge, and pedagogy.

To illustrate: It is not enough for teachers of the English language arts to love literature, to value it as an art form and as a way of understanding the human experience; teachers also need sufficient knowledge of literature which will enable them to introduce students to appropriate traditional and nontraditional texts, and they need the pedagogical knowledge and skills to engage learners in meaningful transactions with literature and to assess students' responses to it. Attitudes, knowledge, and pedagogy are interdependent.

Similarly, it is not enough for teachers of the English language arts to understand and use new technologies; they often must be proficient in troubleshooting problems with VCRs, computers, and laser disc players. They need to recognize the power and potential influences of a range of media, and be able to incorporate and evaluate instructional technology in the language classroom. They need, then, to have the knowledge, the skills, and a positive attitude toward the role of technology in language learning.

The interconnections among attitudes, knowledge, and pedagogy—like the holistic structure of language itself—must be acknowledged and understood by the teacher of English language arts. The chart on the following pages highlights some of those connections by showing how *sets* of items from each of the three areas—attitudes, knowledge, and pedagogy—illustrate the different underlying principles outlined in the first chapter of this document. (The number in parentheses at the end of each entry refers to the numbered entries in the corresponding chapter. There is no one-to-one relationship between the individual items across the three categories.)

CONNECTIONS AMONG PRINCIPLES, ATTITUDES, KNOWLEDGE, AND PEDAGOGY			
PRINCIPLES	**ATTITUDES**	**KNOWLEDGE**	**PEDAGOGY**
Diversity	A recognition that all students can learn and are worthy of a teacher's attention in the English language arts classroom (1). A desire to use the English language arts curriculum to help students become familiar with diverse peoples and cultures (2). A respect and enthusiasm for the individual language, dialect, bi-dialectal competence, and other language variations of each student (3). A willingness to seek a match between students' needs and teachers' objectives, methods, and materials for instruction in English language arts that places students' needs at the center of the curriculum (5). A recognition of the value of diversity of opinion (11).	There is a close relationship between how home language, native language, dialect, and a second language are acquired and developed (2). Social, cultural, and economic environments are intrinsic parts of language learning (4). There is an extensive body of literature and literary genres in English and in translation—including the well-known and the little-known, the commonly used in the curriculum and the rarely used, the traditional and the unusual—representing a worldview appropriate for the classroom (12). Student learning should be described through the use of a variety of assessments (16). There are many versions of English (6).	Create learning environments which promote respect for and understanding of individual academic, ethnic, racial, language, cultural, and gender differences (5). Structure the classroom in a manner that encourages students to work independently and collaboratively (2). Use a variety of materials and media (3). Promote classroom discourse in which student thinking is respected and challenged by the teacher and other students (9). Enrich and expand the learner's language resources for different social and cultural settings (13).
Content Knowledge *Language*	A commitment to continued professional growth in the teaching of the English language arts (7). A conviction that teachers help students grow by encouraging creative and appropriate uses of language (4). A pride in teaching the English language arts and a willingness to take informed stands on issues of professional concern (8). A respect and enthusiasm for the individual language, dialect, bi-dialectal competence, and other language variations of each student (3).	Growth in language is a developmental process (1). The English language is dynamic rather than static (5). There are many versions of English (6). Language and visual images influence thinking and actions (8).	Engage learners in discussion, interpretation, and evaluation of ideas, whether presented in oral, written, or visual form (14). Design instruction that reflects language as a human creation (15). Enrich and expand the learner's language resources for different social and cultural settings (13).
Literature	Appreciation of literature both as an art form and as a means of understanding the human experience (Introduction). A desire to use the English language arts curriculum to help students become familiar with diverse peoples and cultures (2). A commitment to encourage students to read and write about the special insights and feelings they derive from literature (13).	Readers respond to and interpret what they read in a constructive or transactional process (10). Proficient readers consciously create and discover meaning and monitor their own comprehension (11). Literature is a source for exploring and interpreting the experiences of human beings—their achievements, frustrations, foibles, values, and conflicts (13).	Build a reading, listening, and viewing community where students respond, interpret, think critically, and contrast ideas with others (16). Engage learners in transactions with literature (17).

"Connections" chart continued on next page

Continued from previous page			
PRINCIPLES	**ATTITUDES**	**KNOWLEDGE**	**PEDAGOGY**
Composing	Recognition of composing—written, oral, and visual—as a means of discovering self, learning about the world, creating meaning, and sharing with others (Introduction).	There are processes and elements in the act of composing that are crucial to oral, visual, and written discourse (7). Writing is a form of inquiry, reflection, and expression (9).	Promote classroom discourse in which student thinking is respected and challenged by the teacher and other students (9). Enrich and expand the learner's language resources for different social and cultural settings (13). Engage learners in discussion, interpretation, and evaluation of ideas, whether presented in oral, written, or visual form (14). Design instruction that reflects language as a human creation (15).
Media	A willingness to encourage students to respond critically to different media and communications technology (6). A sensitivity to the impact that events and developments in the world outside the school have on teachers, their colleagues, their students, and the English language arts curriculum (9).	Knowledge of the power and the potential of print and nonprint media is necessary to understanding contemporary culture (14). Instructional technology can aid, as well as add to, the English language arts curriculum (15). Language and visual images influence thinking and actions (8).	Promote media literacy (18). Incorporate technology (8). Build a reading, listening, and viewing community where students respond, interpret, think critically, and contrast ideas with others (16).
Pedagogical Knowledge and Skill	A commitment to continued professional growth in the teaching of the English language arts (7). An enthusiasm for developing lifelong habits of mind to facilitate clear thinking and critical judgment (10). A recognition that all students can learn and are worthy of a teacher's attention in the English language arts classroom (1). A conviction that teachers help students grow by encouraging creative and appropriate uses of language (4). A willingness to seek a match between students' needs and teachers' objectives, methods, and materials for instruction in English language arts that places students' needs at the center of the curriculum (5). A sensitivity to the impact that events and developments in the world outside the school have on teachers, their colleagues, their students, and the English language arts curriculum (9).	Speaking, listening, writing, reading, observing, and thinking are interrelated (3). Student learning should be described through the use of a variety of assessments (16). Standardized testing that alone attempts to describe students according to specific scores does not adequately reflect or support students' learning potential (17). Knowledge of major research findings and theory in the content of the discipline and in issues and trends that affect curriculum is essential for creating a productive teaching and learning environment (18). There is an extensive body of literature and literary genres in English and in translation—including the well-known and the little-known, the commonly used in the curriculum and the rarely used, the traditional and the unusual—representing a worldview appropriate for the classroom (12).	Structure English language arts holistically (1). Structure the classroom in a manner that encourages students to work independently and collaboratively (2). Plan interdisciplinary units (4). Stimulate students in an active, mind-engaging process (6). Use student creations as a part of the instructional program (7). Use frequent and immediate feedback to help students construct new understandings and acquire new skills (10). Develop ways to communicate assessment methods and results to different audiences (11). Use assessment outcomes to improve instruction (12). Use a variety of materials and media (3).

"Connections" chart continued on next page

Continued from previous page

PRINCIPLES	ATTITUDES	KNOWLEDGE	PEDAGOGY
Opportunity	A commitment to continued professional growth in the teaching of the English language arts (7). A pride in teaching the English language arts and a willingness to take informed stands on issues of professional concern (8). An enthusiasm for developing lifelong habits of mind to facilitate clear thinking and critical judgment (10). A desire to promote the arts and humanities in the daily lives of all students (12). A recognition of the value of diversity of opinion (11).	The English language is dynamic rather than static (5). There is an extensive body of literature and literary genres in English and in translation—including the well-known and the little-known, the commonly used in the curriculum and the rarely used, the traditional and the unusual—representing a worldview appropriate for the classroom (12). Language and visual images influence thinking and actions (8). Knowledge of the power and the potential of print and nonprint media is necessary to understanding contemporary culture (14). Student learning should be described through the use of a variety of assessments (16). Knowledge of major research findings and theory in the content of the discipline and in issues and trends that affect curriculum is essential for creating a productive teaching and learning environment (18).	Create learning environments which promote respect for and understanding of individual academic, ethnic, racial, language, cultural, and gender differences (5). Structure English language arts holistically (1). Structure the classroom in a manner that encourages students to work independently and collaboratively (2). Use a variety of materials and media (3). Plan interdisciplinary units (4).
Dynamic Literacy	A commitment to continued professional growth in the teaching of the English language arts (7). A sensitivity to the impact that events and developments in the world outside the school have on teachers, their colleagues, their students, and the English language arts curriculum (9). A desire to promote the arts and humanities in the daily lives of all students (12). A commitment to encourage students to read and write about the special insights and feelings they derive from literature (13).	Social, cultural, and economic environments are intrinsic parts of language learning (4). There are processes and elements in the act of composing that are crucial to oral, visual, and written discourse (7). Writing is a form of inquiry, reflection, and expression (9). Readers respond to and interpret what they read in a constructive or transactional process (10).	Plan interdisciplinary units (4). Use student creations as a part of the instructional program (7). Enrich and expand the learner's language resources for different social and cultural settings (13). Engage learners in transactions with literature (17). Build a reading, listening, and viewing community where students respond, interpret, think critically, and contrast ideas with others (16).

Relation of the *Guidelines* to Standards Projects

While these *Guidelines* were being written, numerous professional, public, and private groups were working to formulate national, state, and local standards for English language arts teaching. For example, the National Council of Teachers of English and the International Reading Association were conducting a joint project to identify content standards in language, reading, and writing instruction. Other national standards projects—including those of the Interstate New Teacher Assessment and Support Consortium, the National Board for Professional Teaching Standards, the National Association of State Directors of Teacher Education and Certification, the New Standards Project, the Educational Testing Service, and the College Board Pacesetter Project—were separately trying to identify, among other things, the "informational skills students must know, the methods to help students learn them, and ways to assess achievement," as ETS put it in one of its documents. In addition, many states were simultaneously writing their own standards for English language arts teaching.

As we worked on these *Guidelines,* we also examined various standards reports, some in final form and some as drafts. While we found that the NCTE guidelines included all of the areas and issues addressed in the emerging standards documents, some parts of our *Guidelines*—particularly where reading, writing, speaking, listening, viewing, and thinking are discussed—have benefitted from the language and ideas found in various standards documents. For example, the range of skills we define as necessary for a new teacher to have in order to teach content, to develop students' verbal abilities, to develop multiple literacies, and to develop curricula is consistent with the NCTE/IRA standards. Similarly, NCTE's *Guidelines for the Preparation of Teachers of English Language Arts* emphasize cultural diversity, second language usage, and the reflective teacher's critical reasoning skills, all of which are prominently featured in various other standards frameworks.

NCTE's *Guidelines for the Preparation of Teachers of English Language Arts* defines standards of teacher performance, as do many of the standards projects. For instance, the National Board for Professional Teaching Standards and the Interstate New Teacher Assessment and Support Consortium both offer model standards for beginning teachers. The National Association of State Directors of Teacher Education and Certification provides outcome-based standards written for elementary, middle, and secondary schools; while the "Assessment Criteria" from the Educational Testing Service outline domains and indicators for teacher performance. On the other hand, the NCTE/IRA standards focus on the student, implicitly challenging teachers to discover and to practice ways to help their students achieve the goals defined in the twelve standards of English language arts.

The specific standards articulated in each of the various standards projects all are addressed in either the attitudes, knowledge base, or pedagogy sections of these NCTE *Guidelines*. Consequently, the guidelines constitute a clear framework within which the different standard documents may be compared. What follows is a written summary of five standards projects, and a table that correlates them with the four sets of principles (diversity, content knowledge, pedagogical knowledge, and opportunity for growth) that undergird NCTE's *Guidelines for the Preparation of Teachers of English Language Arts.*

NCTE/IRA STANDARDS

The National Council of Teachers of English and the International Reading Association offered student-centered standards in their *Standards for the English Language Arts* (published in March 1996):

1. Students read a wide range of print and nonprint texts to build an understanding of texts, of themselves, and of the cultures of the United States and the world; to acquire new information; to respond to the needs and demands of society and the workplace; and for personal fulfillment. Among these texts are fiction and nonfiction, classic and contemporary works.

2. Students read a wide range of literature from many periods in many genres to build an understanding of the many dimensions (e.g., philosophical, ethical, aesthetic) of human experience.

3. Students apply a wide range of strategies to comprehend, interpret, evaluate, and appreciate texts. They draw on their prior experience, their interactions with other readers and writers, their knowledge of word meaning and of other texts, their word identification strategies, and their understanding of textual features (e.g., sound–letter correspondence, sentence structure, context, graphics).

4. Students adjust their use of spoken, written, and visual language (e.g., conventions, style, vocabulary) to communicate effectively with a variety of audiences and for different purposes.

5. Students employ a wide range of strategies as they write and use different writing process elements appropriately to communicate with different audiences for a variety of purposes.

6. Students apply knowledge of language structure, language conventions (e.g., spelling and punctuation), media techniques, figurative language, and genre to create, critique, and discuss print and nonprint texts.

7. Students conduct research on issues and interests by generating ideas and questions, and by posing problems. They gather, evaluate, and synthesize data from a variety of sources (e.g., print and nonprint texts, artifacts, people) to communicate their discoveries in ways that suit their purpose and audience.

8. Students use a variety of technological and informational resources (e.g., libraries, databases, computer networks, video) to gather and synthesize information and to create and communicate knowledge.

9. Students develop an understanding of and respect for diversity in language use, patterns, and dialects across cultures, ethnic groups, geographic regions, and social roles.

10. Students whose first language is not English make use of their first language to develop competency in the English language arts and to develop understanding of content across the curriculum.

11. Students participate as knowledgeable, reflective, creative, and critical members of a variety of literacy communities.

12. Students use spoken, written, and visual language to accomplish their own purposes (e.g., for learning, enjoyment, persuasion, and the exchange of information).

INTASC STANDARDS

The standards from the Interstate New Teacher Assessment and Support Consortium (quoted and paraphrased from *Model Standards for Beginning Teacher Licensing and Development,* 1992 draft, pp. 10–30) state that a beginning teacher:

1. understands the central concepts, tools of inquiry, and structures of the discipline.

2. understands how children learn and develop.

3. understands how students differ in their approaches to learning.

4. understands and uses a variety of instructional strategies.

5. uses an understanding of individual and group motivation and behavior to create a positive learning environment.

6. uses knowledge of effective verbal, nonverbal, and media communication techniques to foster learning.

7. plans instruction based upon solid knowledge of subject matter, students, the community, and curriculum goals.

8. understands and uses formal and informal assessment strategies.

9. is a reflexive practitioner who seeks opportunities to grow professionally.

10. fosters relationships with school colleagues, parents, and agencies in the larger community to support students' learning and well being.

NASDTEC STANDARDS

The standards from the National Association of State Directors of Teacher Education and Certification (paraphrased from the booklet *Teacher Performance Assessments: A Comparative View,* published by the Educational Testing Service in 1995) maintain that an effective teacher demonstrates:

1. knowledge of students' readiness for school.
2. knowledge of students' developmental characteristics.
3. knowledge of curriculum.
4. knowledge of instructional strategies.
5. knowledge of multiple assessment methods.
6. knowledge of how to nurture individual and school progress.
7. knowledge of school, home, and community interdependencies.
8. knowledge of ways to integrate technology with instruction.
9. knowledge of support services.
10. knowledge of how to manage educational resources.

NBPTS STANDARDS

The National Board for Professional Teaching Standards developed the following framework for the "Early Adolescence Generalist" (as reported in *Teacher Performance Assessments: A Comparative View,* ETS, 1995):

1. knowledge of early adolescent development, knowledge, skills, values, and other characteristics.
2. knowledge of subject matter.
3. knowledge of varied instructional resources.
4. capacity to engender a caring yet challenging learning environment.
5. willingness to encourage personal, meaningful learning.
6. capacity to help students build knowledge and strengthen understanding.
7. determination to foster social development.
8. capacity to employ a variety of assessment methods.
9. capacity to assess and to strengthen teaching effectiveness.
10. capacity to work in family partnerships.
11. capacity to improve schools, further knowledge, and advance current pedagogy in collaboration with colleagues.

ETS STANDARDS

Finally, the Educational Testing Service, in its "Teacher Performance Assessments," uses domains and indicators to describe the effective teacher as one with significant skills in:

Domain A: Organizing Content Knowledge for Student Learning

1. Becomes familiar with students' background knowledge.
2. Articulates clear learning goals.
3. Demonstrates an understanding of connections between past, current, and possible future content knowledge.
4. Creates and selects appropriate methods, activities, and materials for instruction.
5. Creates or selects appropriate evaluation strategies.

Domain B: Creating an Environment for Student Learning

1. Creates a climate that promotes fairness.
2. Establishes and maintains rapport with students.
3. Communicates challenging learning expectations for each student.
4. Establishes and maintains consistent standards of classroom behavior for students.
5. Makes the physical environment safe and conducive to learning.

Domain C: Teaching for Student Learning

1. Makes learning goals and instructional procedures clear to students.
2. Makes content comprehensible.
3. Encourages students to extend their thinking.
4. Monitors students' understanding of content.
5. Uses instructional time effectively.

Domain D: Teacher Professionalism

1. Reflects on the extent to which the learning goals were met.
2. Demonstrates a sense of efficacy.
3. Builds professional relationships with colleagues.
4. Communicates with parents and caregivers of students.

CORRELATIONS BETWEEN THE *GUIDELINES* AND THE STANDARDS

The following table illustrates how the principles that underlie these *Guidelines* are reflected in the diverse standards projects. As the development of standards for English language arts teachers and students continues, those in the profession will need to stay abreast of the latest findings, contribute ideas whenever possible, and utilize the best suggestions in order to enhance English language arts teaching.

Interrelationships Between the *Guidelines* and Five Standards Projects					
Guidelines	**NCTE/IRA**	**INTASC**	**NASDTEC**	**NBPTS**	**ETS**
Principles of Diversity, 1–5	1–4, 8–12	1–10	1–4, 6–10	1, 7, 10	A: 1, 2, 4 B: 1, 2 C: 1, 2 D: 4
Principles of Content Knowledge, 1–7	1–9, 11	1–8	1–5, 8, 10	2, 7	A: 2, 3, 4 C: 1, 2, 4, 5
Principles of Pedagogical Knowledge/ Skills, 1–3	1–12	1–8, 10	1–10	3–10	A: 2–5 B: 1–5 C: 1–5
Principles of Opportunity, 1–6	1–12	1–10	1–7, 9, 10	7, 9, 11	B: 1, 2, 4, 5 C: 3 D: 3

Guidelines: NCTE's *Guidelines for the Preparation of Teachers of English Language Arts*
NCTE/IRA: National Council of Teachers of English / International Reading Association
INTASC: Interstate New Teacher Assessment and Support Consortium
NASDTEC: National Association of State Directors of Teacher Education and Certification
NBPTS: National Board for Professional Teaching Standards
ETS: Educational Testing Service's "Teacher Performance Assessments"

Characteristics of Effective Teacher-Preparation Programs for English Language Arts

Yearlong Field Experiences in a Major State University

Megastate University is its state's flagship institution. It graduates as many as 125 beginning English teachers each year, and it enjoys a national reputation for doctoral programs in English education.

As a result of an agreement between Megastate and three school systems serving small towns and the countryside, a group of thirty preservice English teachers spends a full year of field-based studies culminating in fifteen weeks of student teaching. They are taught by two full-time university faculty, one of whom is a gifted tenth-grade English teacher with a three-year appointment to Megastate's College of Education faculty.

A New Sequence of Methods Courses

Amos College, which graduates approximately fifty new English teachers each year, is an "up and coming" institution in a major metropolitan area. It has used new faculty to reconceive and revitalize its vision of how to prepare effective teachers of adolescents.

Dissatisfaction with the prior English education program at Amos stimulated eighteen months of collaborative planning between the faculty of the education and English departments. A new program has been in place for a year, in which English faculty assume primary responsibility for teaching a sequence of methods courses in language, literature, and composition. They participate extensively in evaluating student teachers.

Quantity, Quality, and Diversity of Pre-Student Teaching Field Experiences

Lindsay State, a commuter institution serving many first-generation college and nontraditional students, graduates between twenty and thirty beginning English teachers annually. As many as half of Lindsay State's English education majors, already hold B.A. degrees in English or a related field and complete its English education curriculum on a postbaccalaureate basis.

At Lindsay State, a sequence of highly varied field experiences begins in the sophomore year. Before student teaching, preservice English teachers observe or serve as teaching assistants for no fewer than 125 hours in classrooms of English teachers, most of whom have been recommended or selected by the program director.

Aligning Teacher Education Practice with State Reading and Writing Standards

Boswell University, founded as a normal school, evolved by the 1920s into its state's best-known teachers' college, and became a multipurpose regional university thirty years ago. It graduates as many as 100 beginning English teachers annually.

As one dimension of overall educational restructuring, the state in which Boswell is located adopted standards for grades 7–12 English classrooms, so Boswell faculty determined that these standards should provide a rationale for restructuring methods courses. Because all teachers in the state will soon be expected to "align curriculum, instruction, and assessment" in light of new standards, Boswell students center their studies on standards, on instruction which is standards based, and on assessment practices designed to help students display what they know and can do.

Megastate University, Amos College, Lindsay State, and Boswell University are fictional schools, but the vignettes are based on real teacher-preparation programs. We offer these thumbnail sketches of promising or exemplary practices so that other institutions may reflect on, study, or adapt these models for their own college or university. Through the sketches, we want to make clear that many kinds of institutions—those with national reputations and those that are relatively unknown; those serving students who are eighteen to twenty-three years old as well as those with a high proportion of older, nontraditional students; private and public institutions; urban and rural; small private colleges as well as very large universities—can and should aspire to meet these *Guidelines.*

We address this chapter to our colleagues who wish to evaluate existing English teacher-preparation programs, to those who seek ways to improve their programs, and to those charged with designing new curricula for beginning English language arts teachers. This section of the *Guidelines* will also be helpful to those seeking national accreditation of their English language arts programs and to leaders charged with preparing curriculum folios for review by NCTE and for accreditation by the National Council for the Accreditation of Teacher Education (NCATE).

We believe that a strong teacher-preparation program is the product of vision, energy, and sound theory; its faculty includes thoughtful, well-informed educators who continually seek to review and improve the program, finding ways to make it even better. We further believe that these *Guidelines* will help inform the vision of what good English teacher education is all about, and will provide touchstones for department and colleges of education leaders who must make decisions about teacher-preparation curricula.

DIMENSIONS OF EFFECTIVE PROGRAMS FROM THE 1986 *GUIDELINES*

The 1986 *Guidelines* delineated three dimensions that characterized successful preparation programs for teachers of the English language arts: "[They must] provide prospective teachers with models of effective teaching, . . . encourage prospective teachers to analyze the nature of effective teaching, . . . and place prospective teachers in schools where they can observe and practice various aspects of effective teaching" (p. 17). Though numerous changes have shaped educational practice in the past ten years, the qualities of sound preparation programs still include these dimensions. Therefore, we use them to explore the vignettes that open this section. These sketches illustrate that there are many paths to follow in developing preparation programs that meet the guidelines on a point-by-point basis, and that work well in a larger, holistic sense.

Megastate University, through its yearlong professional studies/student-teaching program, attends to each dimension called for in the 1986 *Guidelines*. It selects mentor (cooperating) teachers carefully, and, through a grant program, compensates them fairly for indepth summer training. The program builds in multiple opportunities for analysis of teaching and it provides students with an enviable sequence of opportunities to both observe and practice their craft.

A recent Megastate graduate observes, "I met my mentor teacher for the first time in July. Through yearlong contact with my mentor, and beginning in September, with the juniors my mentor and I taught last year, I feel ready now—truly ready—for being the kind of English teacher kids need and the kind of teacher I want to be."

Amos College, dissatisfied with the apparent gap between teacher educators and professors of literature, language, and composition, decided to give its English faculty a high level of ownership for teacher preparation. Through their school-based experiences and interactions with faculty in the School of Education, English department faculty have refined their own knowledge of skillful teaching of the English language arts. In turn, this knowledge informs and shapes the content of methods courses in literature, language, and composition. As a result, English professors at Amos are increasingly seen as models of effective teaching.

A linguistics professor at Amos comments, "For a number of years, we felt cut off from what the people in teacher education were doing—or maybe 'oblivious' describes things better. Their students took our classes—some were great, some were marginal—but we were unaware of what they, as prospective teachers of English, did beyond that or how they did it. That's all changed now; two colleagues and I planned the new English Education Pedagogy Core, and, along with a full-time field supervisor, we get to see how student teachers put what they learned on campus to the test in the real world."

Lindsay State, a small, centrally located teacher education institution in a community of close to 200,000, has taken advantage of its size to provide an array of superior pre-student teaching field experiences. Each Lindsay student works with two or more cooperating teachers (many of whom are Lindsay State graduates themselves) who provide strong models of effective professional practice. Further, students are given diverse opportunities to build their understanding of learners and learning; for example, they may work with middle-class seventh or eighth graders in one field experience and urban, culturally diverse adolescents during student teaching.

As Lindsay State's English education program director explains, "Our students need the broader view, need to see that good English teaching may occur in any classroom, so we make sure they have a chance to work with younger kids in a middle school, with nominally at-risk kids in either a rural or inner-city school, with the 'brightest and the best'—you name it. They may be reluctant at first, but they return to campus with comments like, 'Hey, this wasn't so bad! Maybe I could get interested in working with the junior high set after all. They're so energetic!' "

Boswell University capitalized on its state's reform movement by participating in it. By emphasizing standards-based teaching—that is, by teaching preservice teachers how to develop lessons and instructional units that are aligned to curriculum standards—Boswell makes sure that its graduates will be among those teachers in the state who accept as a matter of course the alignment of goals, teaching practice, and assessment strategies. In this fashion, Boswell students "analyze the nature of effective teaching" while participating in the systemic reform of educational practice.

A Boswell methods professor observes, "This is dramatically different from the teach–test–reteach by which many of [the students] learned." It is also dramatically different in the sense that only rarely are state departments of education, local systems, and teacher-preparation colleges in step with one another. This professor points out that cooperating teachers are, in general, unfamiliar with standards-based teaching; but through Boswell's program, teacher educators, practicing teachers, and preservice teachers collaborate in developing a realistic understanding of how restructured English language arts teaching can work.

TWO NEW DIMENSIONS OF EFFECTIVE PREPARATION PROGRAMS: LINKING TEACHER EDUCATION, ENGLISH, AND PRACTITIONERS

Successful English language arts preparation programs are frequently linked closely to one or more larger entities in English or education departments. Recognizing the increasing complexity of teacher preparation today, English teacher educators rely less often than in the past on a sequence of English classes, a catch-all methods course, and student teaching to produce well-prepared beginning English teachers. Rather, they form productive partnerships with language and literature faculty, with secondary curriculum specialists, and with professors of learning and human development to enhance programs that otherwise would be strong as much by happenstance as by design.

Amos College, for example, recognized that English faculty had to play a central role in teacher education, and Lindsay State's field-based secondary block program is a fusion of general secondary curriculum studies and English methods. Its secondary curriculum course reinforces developing knowledge of such areas as curriculum restructuring, untracking, technology, and multicultural education.

The second new dimension that the 1996 *Guidelines* identify for effective teacher-preparation programs is providing opportunities for prospective teachers of English to construct their own unique versions of the beginning "English language arts teacher." Increasingly, well-informed teacher educators recognize that when we do our jobs well, students who complete our programs are makers of their own teacher selves, not merely the human products of our lectures or unit requirements or portfolios. Programs that recognize—we might even say *salute*—this principle are characterized by humility on the one hand, and, on the other, by pride and respect for each student's authority over his or her own learning. These programs also do not attempt too much all at once, and they recognize that beginning teachers continue to develop their abilities and insights regarding effective professional practice.

Megastate University's program of extensive field-based studies illustrates this point. Through these experiences, preservice English teachers may test, reconsider, and refine what they "know" of skillful teaching in an environment of real teachers, real students, and real schools. And Lindsay State students, through courses rich in collaboration and well-conceived projects later used in student teaching, are, in the words of its *English Education Student Handbook*, encouraged to "make their own teacher."

REVIEWING TEACHER-PREPARATION PROGRAMS: THE NCTE-NCATE CONNECTION

In *How English Teachers Get Taught* (published by NCTE in 1995), Peter Smagorinsky and Melissa Whiting analyzed eighty-one syllabi for undergraduate English methods courses and found that the 1986 *Guidelines* "permeated, in one way or another, most of the syllabi" (p. 101). Institutions seeking accreditation from NCATE (National Council for the Accreditation of Teacher Education) are given the opportunity to have their English teacher-preparation programs reviewed by NCTE. (For a complete description of the connection between NCTE and NCATE, see the *Handbook for Preparing the NCTE/NCATE Folio in English Language Arts,* published by NCTE.)

Since 1988, teams of NCTE members have evaluated many English education curriculum folios prepared by American colleges and universities. Folio reviewers have found many programs in compliance with the NCTE *Guidelines* on their first submission; many others have, on a second or third submission, been found in compliance with those guidelines. Through the folio review process, some major universities have discovered that in order to meet the profession's current expectations for teachers of English language arts, changes must be made, new courses designed, and ways found to offer substantive laboratory and clinical experiences at the pre-student teaching level. Already folio reviewers report that courses addressing adolescent literature, multicultural literature, literature by women, nonprint media study, and composition methods—all areas emphasized both in the 1986 and now in the 1996 *Guidelines*—are far more likely to be required of prospective teachers of the English language arts than they were in the mid-1980s. Folio reviewers have also found numerous small institutions (those serving as few as a thousand students and with as few as three or four English education graduates annually) that have been remarkably resourceful in finding ways to implement program components which meet the criteria set forth in the *Guidelines*.

We believe that structuring teacher-preparation programs in accordance with the principles and objectives contained in these *Guidelines* will improve instruction for English education majors, and ultimately, for the students those preservice instructors will teach.

Effective Transition to Teaching

EDITOR'S NOTE: The Commission on Transition to Teaching was formed by the Conference on English Education in 1988 to explore the areas of student teaching and induction as they applied to the English language arts. The commission sponsored a number of open meetings and sessions to invite comment and assistance from the membership of CEE and of the National Council of Teachers of English in general.

This chapter—which originally appeared as an article in the October 1992 issue of English Education, *published by NCTE—represents the commission's recommended guidelines. It is divided into two major sections: student teaching and induction of beginning English language arts teachers. (The original article in* English Education *also included a bibliography of resources beginning teachers might find helpful; that listing has been omitted here.)*

The original article was developed by an editorial subcommittee of the CEE commission, consisting of Charles R. Duke, chair; Daniel J. Cox, Lela M. Detoye, Bonnie Ericson, Rebecca Farris, Joan F. Kaywell, Sharon Kingen, Michael T. Moore, Elizabeth Poe, Sam Robinson, and Alan B. Teasley. The editorial subcommittee was helped by these consultant readers: Rita Brause, Nancy Lester, Carol Luckenbach, John Mayher, Diana Mitchell, Ann Renninger, Mary Ann Rudy, and Ken Spurlock.

INTRODUCTION

The first section addresses the student teaching experience. These recommendations are based on the assumption that the preservice teacher has had a solid foundation of preparation as outlined in NCTE's 1986 *Guidelines for the Preparation of Teachers of English Language Arts*. As the *Guidelines* recommend, preservice teacher education programs for English language arts should provide a full range of field experiences. These experiences, which should occur throughout the preparation program, ought to be developmental in nature, provide instructional and psychological support, and offer realistic, practical class-room experiences leading naturally into the student teaching experience.

Student teaching programs in English language arts—whether elementary or second-ary, whether large or small, whether traditional or experimental—must meet three basic goals: (1) provide realistic teaching experiences which call for the student teacher to dem-onstrate both the breadth and depth of his or her knowledge of English language arts and effective pedagogical skills; (2) encourage the student teacher's continuing professional development; and (3) foster a sense of professionalism and collegiality and nurture teacher–student relations.

To accomplish these goals, teacher education units and cooperating school districts must work together to assess student abilities in such areas as knowledge of content, knowl-edge of learners, knowledge of pedagogy, implementation of integrated English language arts curricula, understanding of the school milieu, knowledge about and skill with class-room management techniques, implementation of a variety of teaching strategies, and knowl-edge about the teaching profession. Ideally, the teacher education faculty and district per-sonnel—especially the field supervisor and cooperating teacher—establish meaningful re-lationships of trust with student teachers, forming a network of support and collegiality through which the student teacher is ensured opportunities for professional growth and continuing professional development.

The second section of this document focuses upon induction, the transition from stu-dent teaching to the first years of full-time teaching. This period of induction has become increasingly important because of the high rate of attrition among teachers in their first years of experience. Over 50 percent of the teaching profession leaves the classroom within the first seven years. Many of the reasons for this high departure rate can be traced to the initial years of teaching during which the novice teacher often experienced problems and had little or no support for addressing them and finding appropriate solutions. Even with strong student teaching experiences, beginning English language arts teachers face difficult challenges: integrating the teaching of a variety of literary works; overseeing students' varied composing processes; promoting language and thinking skills; coping with the paper load; and, of course, handling the inevitable classroom management and discipline issues which arise.

Unlike many professions in which the expectations are that the individual will move through a transition period of continued support and education, most English language arts teachers work in isolation throughout the beginning of their careers. In fact, teaching is one of the few professions where the beginning teacher is expected to have the same level of skill and knowledge as that of the experienced and successful one. Not having the advan-tage of an apprentice system or even regular collaboration with colleagues, beginning teachers often must fend for themselves and frequently in such cases never realize their full poten-tial; instead, they may develop survival skills which may enable them to continue but not necessarily grow as professionals.

School districts, teacher education units, and professional organizations such as NCTE and its affiliates share the responsibility for making certain that beginning English language arts teachers receive the support they need to accomplish a successful transition to independent full-time teaching. The major responsibility in an induction support system must be assumed by the district or school; it is, after all, the district which does the hiring and controls the amount and type of information given to new teachers, the teaching assignment, the curriculum, and the evaluation procedures.

But districts and schools are not solely responsible. The majority of teacher education programs operate on the assumption that once the student graduates, the program's responsibility ends. However, the program does have a continuing responsibility to its graduates, whether it be follow-up support in the field or continued revision and refinement of its program to ensure better-prepared English language arts teachers once they are practicing in the field. And although professional organizations such as NCTE and its affiliates may not be directly involved in the support of beginning English language arts teachers, participation in such organizations has proven helpful to new teachers who find there additional support networks and a sense of collegiality. As a result, professional organizations need to find ways to encourage this participation.

Carefully designed student teaching and induction programs, when viewed as integral parts of an extended, professional development process, and when supported by teacher education programs, school districts, and professional organizations, should lead to increased retention, improved attitudes toward English language arts teaching, and a new generation of capable and inspiring English language arts teachers.

The CEE Commission on Transition to Teaching intends that these suggested guidelines will be discussed by teacher educators, cooperating teachers, department chairs, principals, and others in the schools whose responsibilities may relate to student teachers and beginning teachers. The Commission also hopes that these guidelines stimulate professional organizations dedicated to serving English language arts teachers into becoming more directly involved in the experiences of both student teachers and the new teacher. In particular, the Commission hopes that all these individuals and groups will work collaboratively to ensure a continuum of early field, student teaching, and beginning teacher experiences which offers strong collegial support for the ongoing professional growth and development of the English language arts teacher.

PART I: GUIDELINES FOR THE STUDENT TEACHING EXPERIENCE IN ENGLISH LANGUAGE ARTS

Beginning teachers repeatedly have cited their student teaching experiences as the most helpful part of their teacher-preparation programs. For most, student teaching represents the culmination of all coursework and other requirements and comes closest to representing in their minds what "real" teachers do. The hands-on nature of the student-teaching experience, the interaction with students for an extended period of time, the relationships with cooperating teachers and teacher education supervisors in the field, all remain vividly imprinted in the memories of most teachers.

Programmatic Characteristics

Effective student teaching programs in English language arts are based upon well-established guidelines and relationships between teacher education programs and schools. These guidelines and relationships have been mutually agreed upon by the schools and teacher education units who continually monitor them for effectiveness. A process exists whereby changes can be made after appropriate consultation. Guidelines address issues such as placement procedures, cooperating teacher qualifications, rights and responsibilities of all parties, and the nature of evaluation. Ideally, an advisory council or committee comprised of representatives from the teacher education unit and the schools work collaboratively to develop such guidelines and procedures and meet on a regular basis to ensure continued articulation. The NCTE *Guidelines for the Preparation of Teachers of English Language Arts* (1986) should be a helpful resource for this process.

The English Language Arts Student Teaching Experience

1. The English language arts student teaching experience, regardless of format, should be an extensive, intensive experience which provides student teachers with authentic opportunities to:

A. Apply their knowledge of content, learners, and pedagogy.

B. Experience an integrated English language arts curriculum.

C. Write and implement their own teaching plans and units and evaluate their effectiveness.

D. Experiment with a variety of teaching strategies and reflect on their outcome, particularly as they relate to the development of a student-centered curriculum in English language arts.

E. Work with and appreciate the needs and contributions of students of differing abilities, socioeconomic levels, and cultural and ethnic backgrounds, while also understanding how these factors affect students' development of literacy.

F. Consider how to determine students' learning and to identify crucial learning goals.

G. Meet regularly for focused, intensive sessions with cooperating teachers to review performance and discuss plans.

H. Examine materials and resources available in the school and community which support the effective teaching of English language arts.

I. Observe cooperating teachers and other classroom teachers as they are teaching and have ample opportunity to discuss the observations with the individuals involved.

J. Learn about the work of other teachers and personnel and participate in meetings, conferences, and inservice with other teachers.

K. Participate in co-curricular activities and other school functions to gain an understanding of the full scope of a school's operation and mission.

L. Meet formally and informally with other student teachers to foster collegiality and a support network.

M. Reflect on their own increased proficiency as teachers.

2. Evaluation and assessment of student teachers should reflect the philosophy that the student teaching experience provides students with *basic* education and preparation as teachers. They are beginning teachers who will continue to develop their professional competence throughout their careers. Evaluation and assessment of the student teaching experience should be based on students having exhibited specific teaching behaviors as well as having exhibited certain professional characteristics during the experience. An effective evaluation and assessment system for English language arts student teachers, therefore, will do the following:

A. Provide clear expectations for the roles and performance by student teachers, cooperating teachers, and teacher education supervisors.

B. Provide for student teacher, cooperating teacher, and teacher education supervisor to set goals collaboratively which fit within the overall expectations for the student teaching experience.

C. Provide for frequent observation and feedback by cooperating teachers and teacher education supervisors.

D. Familiarize student teachers with appropriate district and/or state mandated evaluation expectations and procedures.

E. Examine student teaching portfolios which include samples of tests, assignments, project instructions, etc., constructed by student teachers, as well as samples of their students' work.

F. Document student growth and development.

Professional Relationships

An effective model for a student teaching program will have clearly defined roles for all participants in the program and will encourage the establishment of productive relationships among these participants. The most crucial relationships are those among the cooperating teacher, the teacher education supervisor, and the student teacher. Student teachers usually understand the importance of effective relationships, but they must balance several of these at one time: those with their students (who may or may not consider them a "real" teacher); those with their cooperating teachers (who may or may not consider them colleagues); and those with their teacher education supervisors (who may or may not emphasize the role of advocate more than evaluator).

Effective teachers are those who are able to establish meaningful relationships of mutual respect with students and colleagues. Student teachers need to be encouraged to pursue the development of such relationships. Some student teachers may need more assistance than others in developing the interpersonal skills necessary to ensure that collegial relationships evolve smoothly. A clear definition of roles and expectations in these relationships helps facilitate their development.

The English Language Arts Cooperating Teacher

1. Cooperating teachers should be master teachers who are able to foster with student teachers collegial, collaborative relationships that promote continued personal and professional growth. Effective cooperating teachers for student teachers of English language arts will:

A. Indicate a willingness to serve as a cooperating teacher and to accept the corresponding responsibilities.

B. Hold a valid state certificate in the area for which they supervise.

C. Have a minimum of three years successful teaching experience in the area(s) and/or level for which student teachers are assigned.

D. Show evidence of continued professional development through participation in such opportunities as district inservice, professional meetings, master's programs, and membership in appropriate organizations, etc.

E. Exhibit exemplary teaching skills which serve as a model for student teachers.

F. Express a willingness to participate in training for student teacher supervision.

G. Exhibit a willingness to work cooperatively with teacher education personnel.

H. Be familiar with the content of the student teacher's preparation program.

I. Possess a working knowledge of any state or district mandated evaluation instrument and be trained in its use.

J. Be an active member of NCTE and an appropriate affiliate.

2. Effective cooperating teachers will understand appropriate supervision and evaluation techniques approved by the district and teacher education program. Understanding the purposes of supervision and evaluation, effective cooperating teachers will accept and carry out the following tasks:

A. Define the cooperating teacher's expectations for English language arts student teachers.

B. Familiarize student teachers with the community, district, school, and classroom milieu and protocols.

C. Assist in the transition from student to classroom teacher of English language arts.

D. Introduce student teachers as professionals to colleagues and to classroom students.

E. Be certain student teachers have a work area and necessary materials, as well as a preparation period for studying, planning, and evaluation.

F. Establish collaboratively with student teachers an overall plan for the teaching experience.

G. Facilitate gradual induction of student teachers into teaching and related responsibilities.

H. Provide modeling of successful instructional and management techniques with ample time for follow-up discussion and reflection.

I. Help student teachers develop competencies related to successful teaching of English language arts.

J. Provide regular formative feedback focusing on the performance of student teachers.

K. Confer regularly with student teachers to provide ideas, answer questions, and encourage experimentation and creativity.

L. Confer regularly with teacher education supervisors about student teachers' performance and participate in joint conferences with student teachers and supervisors.

M. Provide both oral and written evaluative feedback as requested by the teacher education program.

The English Language Arts Teacher Education Supervisor

1. Teacher education supervisors of student teachers in English language arts serve as both advocate and evaluator and provide the bridge between school district and the teacher education program. To function effectively in this role, supervisors will:

A. Have recent comparable and successful school-based teaching experience in the area(s) and/or levels for which student teachers are assigned.

B. Have specific preparation in supervising student teachers.

C. Possess genuine interest in elementary, middle, and/or secondary education.

D. Be mentor-teachers with a desire to continue their own learning as they work with student teachers.

E. Participate in the design and implementation of the preparation program in English language arts and its continued evaluation and redesign.

F. Be knowledgeable about resources available to support the teaching of English language arts.

G. Possess personal warmth balanced with an insistence on quality.

H. Be an active member of NCTE and an appropriate affiliate.

I. Be familiar with area schools, programs, and personnel and show respect for their efforts.

J. Possess ability to maintain poise and professionalism in conflict situations.

K. Possess effective listening skills and ability to respond.

L. Be acquainted with student teacher(s) and their backgrounds prior to supervision.

2. Effective teacher education supervisors need to be acutely aware of relationships as they exist and be capable of influencing the development of relationships between student teachers and cooperating teachers and between student teachers and students. To foster such relationships, teacher education supervisors will accept and carry out the following responsibilities:

A. Foster an awareness among student teachers of the importance of interpersonal relationships in building trust and respect between teacher and students and how such relationships contribute to learning.

B. Establish a relationship which encourages ongoing open communication among student teachers, cooperating teachers, and the teacher education supervisor.

C. Clarify the expectations of the teacher education program for student teachers and cooperating teachers.

D. Work collaboratively with cooperating teachers and school and district personnel to provide realistic, relevant experiences for English language arts student teachers.

E. Serve as a resource for both student teachers and cooperating teachers.

F. Ensure adherence to program requirements.

G. Maintain a flexible schedule which permits frequent and varied visitations/observations.

H. Schedule and use conference time appropriately with both student teachers and cooperating teachers for intensive, extended discussion.

I. Provide frequent and effective written and oral feedback to student teachers.

J. Provide ample opportunities for feedback from cooperating teachers.

K. Complete conscientious, insightful, thorough, and well-documented evaluations after appropriate collaborative consultation with cooperating teachers and student teachers.

The English Language Arts Student Teacher

1. Prior to entering the student teaching experience, student teachers in English language arts should have demonstrated a basic competency level of skill and knowledge in the following areas (consult *Guidelines for the Preparation of Teachers of English Language Arts* for a fuller discussion):

A. Language development, writing, reading, listening, speaking, viewing, literature, and media.

B. Communication, both oral and written.

C. Instructional planning, classroom management, discipline, and student assessment.

D. Knowledge about learning styles and students' special needs and which affect literacy development.

E. Knowledge of the content and processes involved in the teaching of English language arts.

F. Knowledge of current trends in the teaching of English language arts.

G. Knowledge of the expectations related to improving students' skills in speaking, listening, reading, writing, viewing, and critical thinking.

H. Knowledge of the role of the integrated language arts curriculum in fostering student learning.

I. Participation in early field and clinical work which focuses on understanding: the school environment; the relationship of English language arts to other content areas; the effects of classroom climate, management, and teaching styles and strategies on fostering learning; the administrative arrangement and operation within a school and district; and the procedures and availability of services and resources.

2. English language arts student teachers must expect to accept a dual role during the student teaching experience. On the one hand, they are still part of the teacher education program and therefore must continue, to some extent, in a student role; on the other hand, they must function effectively within the school district and school as an emerging professional with corresponding duties and responsibilities. The expectations within this latter role include the following:

A. Become familiar with the community, school, and individual learners.

B. Become familiar with school schedules, curriculum facilities, and personnel.

C. Become familiar with and carry out district policies.

D. Report promptly and regularly to teaching and related duties.

E. Complete all assignments in a timely and thorough manner.

F. Display a comprehensive knowledge of English language arts.

G. Prepare and teach daily lesson plans as well as appropriate unit and long-term plans and evaluate their effectiveness during the term of student teaching.

H. Develop and use instructional materials effectively.

I. Model effective oral and written communication.

J. Share responsibility with cooperating teachers for providing meaningful learning experiences for students.

K. Create a classroom atmosphere which encourages learning and student involvement.

L. Be an appropriate role model for students.

M. Pursue suggestions from all support personnel to ensure professional growth.

N. Observe cooperating teachers and others in the assigned school.

O. Confer regularly with cooperating teachers and teacher education supervisors.

P. Meet regularly with other student teachers to foster a collaborative learning and support network.

Q. Assist teachers with co-curricular activities.

R. Attend professional meetings, parent conferences, and school functions.

S. Display and practice initiative, fairness, and professional behavior.

T. Maintain confidentiality when expected.

U. Become increasingly responsible for each student's learning.

V. Exemplify the teaching profession's highest standards of ethical conduct.

PART II: GUIDELINES FOR THE INDUCTION OF BEGINNING ENGLISH LANGUAGE ARTS TEACHERS

Most teachers, reflecting on their beginning year or two of teaching, will indicate that the transition from teacher-preparation student to full-time professional was not easy. Although students may have gone through outstanding English language arts teacher-preparation programs, including highly successful student teaching experiences, entering the full-time world of teaching and finding the challenges which lie therein can still be a shock. In the past, new teachers were given a teaching assignment and left to find the most effective, or expedient, means for surviving—a simple case of sink-or-swim.

Fortunately, increasing numbers of teacher-preparation programs, school districts, and professional organizations have recognized the problems of beginning teachers and have moved to provide a smoother and more professional transition. Many states now mandate induction programs or beginning teacher assistance programs to provide a framework within which the novice can find answers for many questions as well as collegiality and support.

Beginning English language arts teachers have a number of needs which must be met if the transition into full-time teaching is to be successful. School districts, teacher education preparation programs, and professional organizations share the responsibility for meeting these needs. Efforts should start even before beginning teachers step into classrooms on the first day and should continue through the initial years of teaching until the new teachers feel comfortable in their new role and understand how the induction support network operates. This can best be accomplished by the establishment of common goals among the three groups.

The Teacher-Preparation Program

The preparation for this transition into teaching begins with the teacher education program responsible for training new English language arts teachers. If the program reflects the characteristics outlined in *Guidelines for the Preparation of Teachers of English Language Arts,* the transition should be smooth. The English language arts teacher-preparation program, however, should be organized to provide assistance before an individual teacher receives his or her first teaching position and then to provide continuing assistance and support throughout the first, and perhaps subsequent years, of teaching.

1. Prior to any of its graduates being hired, the English language arts teacher-preparation program should:

A. Know it reflects the most current research and practice and meets NCTE guidelines.

B. Guarantee it has strong linkages with schools by developing school-based development programs.

C. Have faculty who are regularly involved with public schools and who understand the demands placed on beginning teachers.

D. Bring former "new" English language arts teachers on campus regularly to discuss with students expectations about their first teaching position.

E. Provide prospective English language arts teachers with practice in interviewing, advice on developing placement files, and assistance in obtaining information about certification policies in states where graduates might teach.

F. Publicize current listings of available English language arts teaching positions.

G. Provide information about NCTE and other professional organizations.

2. The English language arts teacher-preparation program as a regular practice should:

A. Assist school districts with the education of English language arts mentors and with the development of appropriate supervisory approaches for all personnel directly involved with beginning English language arts teachers.

B. Make initial contact with its graduates to determine such information as their teaching assignments and location, and communicate that information to appropriate teacher education faculty.

C. Establish a visitation schedule for teacher education faculty whenever possible; such visitations should be for formative purposes only and not linked to any ongoing district evaluation program. Visits should be approved by the school district and the beginning teacher as a regular procedure.

D. Hold a series of informal meetings on and/or off campus in which new English language arts teachers, mentors, and teacher education faculty can discuss English language arts issues and concerns.

E. Foster the development of novice support groups among new English language arts teachers.

F. Be available for on-site consultation with school district personnel and the new teacher if difficulties arise.

G. Sponsor inservice seminars that encourage discussion and reflection about new approaches and trends in English language arts.

H. Encourage districts to adopt a gradual immersion policy for new teachers, providing limited teaching assignments and class size until the new teacher becomes successfully established.

I. Conduct follow-up surveys and visits to determine from both new English language arts teachers and their administrators how program graduates are doing; relate findings back to the preparation program and make appropriate adjustments.

J. Encourage new English language arts teachers as well as their mentors to participate in further professional development through such opportunities as master's degree programs and National Writing Project institutes.

K. Recognize and reward appropriately the involvement of program faculty in teaching, supervision, and inservice activity.

The School District

The principal responsibility for insuring that beginning English language arts teachers are successful lies with the districts who hire them. If districts have looked carefully at the needs of new teachers and developed coherent yet flexible plans for dealing with these needs, most beginning teachers will have a productive experience and become a valuable addition to the teaching profession. To guarantee that the transition is as smooth as possible and that the needs of the beginning teacher are addressed, considerable preparation by the district is necessary. Assistance programs need not only to mesh with what new teachers bring with them as a result of their training but also need to prepare these same teachers for continued professional growth, even once they have moved beyond any formal assistance program. Although most assistance programs focus on the first year of teaching, no time limit should exist for offering assistance. Different teachers take different periods of time to reach professional maturity and the necessary independence before they can accept and carry out their professional responsibilities. Even the most proficient teachers need to collaborate with professional colleagues to sustain growth and development during their professional careers.

Meeting the Need for Support

Beginning English language arts teachers need both informational and emotional support as they face the unique challenges of teaching. This support can take a number of forms, but the most significant element is undoubtedly the matching of the new teacher with an appropriate mentor or support teacher in the district. The existence of an effective mentoring program is essential to retaining promising new teachers in English language arts, and the selection of experienced teachers who might serve as mentors is central to the success of any district's assistance program. A mentor selection committee, comprised of teachers and administrators who also monitor the effectiveness of the matches between mentors and beginning teachers, is an ideal method for addressing this need.

1. English language arts mentors should be teachers who have:
    A. Considerable teaching experience in English language arts and at the grade levels appropriate for the assignment.
    B. Documented evidence of outstanding teaching ability and performance.
    C. Evidence of respect from peers for their professionalism.

D. Evidence of continuing professional development and growth (i.e., advanced study, activity in professional organizations).

E. Interest in working with beginning teachers and a willingness to accept the responsibility of mentoring.

2. English language arts mentors should receive periodic education and updates that reflect:

A. Understanding of adult learning styles.

B. Effective communication skills.

C. Current knowledge and practice for teaching English language arts.

D. Current knowledge and practice in effective supervision.

3. The "match" between beginning teachers and mentors should be based upon:

A. Similar teaching assignments (i.e., grade level, subject area).

B. Proximity to each other in terms of classrooms and teaching schedules.

C. Similarity in teaching styles, personalities, and educational philosophy.

D. Joint agreement between new teacher and mentor about the appropriateness of the match.

4. In providing assistance to new English language arts teachers, mentors should:

A. Assist new teachers in addressing their professional needs in a systematic fashion (i.e., long-term goal setting for individual students and their specific short-term projects to reach these goals; classroom management; handling the paper load; evaluating student work; locating resources).

B. Serve as role models and support people.

C. Interpret the school culture.

D. Serve as liaison to other faculty who may have expertise to assist the beginning teacher.

E. Meet regularly with new teachers to discuss progress, identify strengths and weaknesses, and provide resources.

Meeting the Need for Time

One of the greatest needs of beginning English language arts teachers is time. The change of pace that the new teacher experiences is one which usually calls for a period of adjustment. Most new teachers report that they never seem to catch up with the work; they rarely have time enough to plan adequately, to respond to student papers, to engage in meaningful dialogue with colleagues or pursue professional development.

1. To ensure that new English language arts teachers have sufficient time to address their needs, a district should:

A. Provide a teaching assignment which initially has a reduced number of different preparations or classes.

B. Assign a balanced mixture of students, having neither all of the advanced nor all of the more troublesome.

C. Ensure a teaching schedule which permits time for consultation with a mentor, including common planning periods.

D. Assign new teachers to their own classrooms.

E. Provide opportunities to attend professional seminars, visit other classrooms, and secure additional perspectives on the teaching of English language arts.

F. Provide an effective match that is agreed upon cooperatively between new teacher and mentor.

G. Limit amounts of extracurricular work.

Meeting the Need for Information

Beginning English language arts teachers need large amounts of information, but this information cannot be presented or absorbed all at the same time. Information about school policies, the community, the English language arts curriculum and instructional practices, evaluation, and other topics have to be provided from many sources within the district or school and this information will be needed at different times during the school year. Providing the right information in the right amount of detail at the right time becomes an important district contribution to assist the first-year teacher.

1. When interviewing prospective new English language arts teachers, the district should provide:

A. An accurate summary of the school and district's demographics, including an unbiased perspective on the community's social, political, and cultural contexts.

B. An overview of the district's English language arts curriculum and policies.

C. An interview with the head teacher, department chair, or other individual charged with responsibility for English language arts.

D. A tour of school facilities.

E. Opportunities to talk with experienced English language arts teachers employed in the district.

F. An explanation of the district's beginning teacher assistance program.

G. An indication of anticipated teaching responsibilities, including a tentative teaching schedule.

2. Prior to the beginning of school, new English language arts teachers should receive:

A. Accurate teaching schedules.

B. Copies of pertinent district curricula and textbooks.

C. Identification of mentors and opportunities to meet with them before school starts.

D. An orientation to the school and its policies and procedures.

E. An orientation to the beginning teacher assistance or induction program.

F. Clear explanation of professional responsibilities, including evaluation procedures and contractual obligations.

G. Identification of and access to professional resources within the district.

H. Access to assigned classroom(s).

3. Once school begins, the district should be certain that the new English language arts teacher has:

A. Regular meetings with mentors who have released time for this purpose.

B. Opportunities for interaction with other teachers in English language arts and in other subject areas.

C. An understanding of formative and summative evaluation for students and teachers as used by the district.

D. Opportunities to become involved with curriculum review, textbook adoption, and other activities related to English language arts.

E. Encouragement to attend professional meetings and inservice.

F. Opportunities to provide feedback about the district's assistance program.

G. Recognition for innovative and/or outstanding work and assistance in launching new ideas.

4. At the end of the school year, the district should arrange to provide beginning English language arts teachers with:

A. An assessment of their performance.

B. An opportunity to discuss the effectiveness of the district's assistance or induction program.

C. An assurance of continued support if the teachers are to remain employed for a second year.

D. An opportunity to reflect on practice and to set goals for improvement in subsequent years.

The Professional Organization

Beginning English language arts teachers may not always realize that professional organizations such as NCTE and its affiliates are another means of support for making the transition from student to full-time professional. To assist the beginning teacher in discovering how important involvement in such organizations can be, the organizations themselves must reach out to new teachers and make a special effort to acquaint them with what the organizations can provide.

1. Professional organizations should take an active role in becoming part of the professional preparation experience for English language arts teachers; this can be accomplished if the organization will:

A. Make certain that English language arts teacher-preparation programs have current materials which accurately describe the purposes and services of the organization.

B. Encourage members to speak in teacher education classes about current issues and practices in the teaching of English language arts.

C. Sponsor on campus, in cooperation with the teacher education program, a group which provides formal recognition for students preparing to teach English language arts.

D. Encourage English language arts teacher-preparation programs to bring groups of prospective teachers to professional meetings and inservice presentations.

E. Provide sessions/workshops at conferences designed solely for the beginning English language arts teacher.

F. Offer student discounts for membership in the organization and purchase of organization materials.

2. Professional organizations need to become a part of the support network for beginning teachers; this can be accomplished if the organizations will:

A. Identify new English language arts teachers in each school and provide a list of these to local organization members in the same district who can then establish personal communication and a local network.

B. Send free samples of its publications and provide introductory "first-year" memberships at reduced prices.

C. Encourage new English language arts teachers to submit proposals for conference sessions; collaboration with a mentor on such a proposal is a good way to begin.

D. Invite new English language arts teachers to become active on local affiliate committees.

E. Establish scholarships/awards for new English language arts teachers to defray the cost of attending conferences.

F. Offer special sessions/workshops designed to meet the needs and interests of beginning teachers.

SUMMARY

No one group or institution can provide all the support that new and experienced English language arts teachers need. Instead, a coalition of the school district, the teacher-preparation program, and the professional organizations dedicated to identifying and retaining quality individuals in the English language arts teaching profession is necessary. The creation of a professional and supportive environment in which English language arts teachers can do what they do best, teach young people about the power and richness which language and literature bring to each person's life, is an investment that cannot be ignored.

Inservice Education: Ten Principles

EDITOR'S NOTE: These principles were originally developed by the 1989–1991 CEE Commission on Inservice Education: Richard Larson, Chair; Barbara Cambridge, Bonnie Chambers, Ken Kantor, Dawn Latta, Nancy Lester, Helen Poole, Gary Salvner, Mary Jo Wagner, and C. Anne Webb. This article first appeared in the May 1994 issue of English Education, *published by the National Council of Teachers of English.*

PREAMBLE

With these principles, the Conference on English Education offers a vision of inservice education that differentiates it from training in teaching techniques and from the occasional, sporadic offering of disconnected workshops. Instead, inservice education is viewed as a major element in a lifelong process by which teachers grow professionally through reflective practice. We affirm that teachers, like other professionals, build new knowledge and revise current beliefs through experiences, reading, discussion, reflection, and interaction with colleagues. Teaching is both an art and a craft—one that, however long a person may practice it, is never perfected.

These axioms of human professional development are the foundations of our view of inservice education. All of the principles that follow are built upon these axioms and invite a vigorous and sustained commitment to professional development by all in the educational community. We offer these principles as a "Bill of Rights" for teachers participating in inservice education—an elucidation of how teachers and administrators alike ought to view the processes of inservice education—and as guidelines for those who are leaders of inservice education programs.

PRINCIPLE ONE: REFLECTIVE PRACTICE

Teachers engage in action and reflection, thus affirming that learning is the key to better teaching. Reflection that is conscious and shared in a professional community provides the necessary context for actively questioning, assessing, and reenvisioning processes of teaching and the beliefs underlying them. Knowledge gained from reflection on (1) the connection between practice and beliefs, (2) the contexts in which learning occurs, (3) the effects of specific teaching practices, and (4) an expanded range of alternative practices encourages teachers to forge integrated theories and approaches to teaching and learning. And as teachers better understand both the constraints imposed and the possibilities offered by the institutions in which they work, they relax the bonds of those constraints and turn possibilities into realities.

PRINCIPLE TWO: OWNERSHIP

Change cannot be forced. Teachers have the prerogative to change or not change their practices in light of what occurs in inservice education. Genuine change is made only when teachers decide for themselves that it is desirable and attainable. Therefore, inservice education provides experiences in a risk-accepting environment where sufficient time and guidance supports teachers to (1) try out alternative ways of teaching and learning, (2) reflect upon those experiences, (3) examine consciously and collaboratively what they attempted, attained, and learned, (4) evaluate what occurred, (5) examine their beliefs and their practices, and (6) decide whether to alter their beliefs and practices.

PRINCIPLE THREE: THEORIZED PRACTICE

The common demand for "practical" inservice education does not obscure the theoretical basis of pedagogy. Inservice education respects teachers' practices while it uncovers the theoretical assumptions underlying them. It treats teachers' concern with "what to do on Monday" as a source of critical issues and questions, not as a call for instant solutions. Such connections encourage assessing assumptions about teaching and learning as they are affected by current theoretical scholarship and by qualitative and quantitative research. When teachers are knowledgeable about how researchers and theorists identify and investigate teaching and learning issues, they are able to assess how those investigations contribute to informed practices and, in turn, to use those assessments to evaluate the effectiveness to their practices. Inservice education can help teachers participate in the full process of scholarly investigation and continue to reflect on the influences contributing to theorized practice.

PRINCIPLE FOUR: COLLABORATION

Collaborating in decision making, negotiating meanings, and sharing explorations build communal visions of teaching and learning. Inservice education does not, therefore, simply deliver information selected by other parties nor impose a packaged set of "changes." Instead, it inspires and maintains an environment in which all who participate work together to investigate issues and questions they have identified as important.

PRINCIPLE FIVE: AGENCY

Collaborative inservice education, to be sure, raises the issue of authority. It poses the questions: "Who is in charge?" and "Who makes the decisions about the focus and timing of inservice programs?" If teachers are to take and retain responsibility for their own learning, they need to take an active role in deciding (1) what to explore in order to grow professionally and (2) how to conduct those explorations. Teachers need to come to an agreement among themselves on the kinds of inservice education they would like their school to arrange and then negotiate with appropriate persons in the larger school community to develop the program.

PRINCIPLE SIX: SUFFICIENT TIME

For any learner, significant learning requires time. Change is a process, not an event. Although training can be given quickly, genuine learning is not hastily achieved. When reflective practitioners question their beliefs and practices, they need time to do so. This is a recursive process: While investigations of one's beliefs are continuing, questions arise, new problems are identified, tentative solutions are considered, and then more questions arise. Inservice education must be planned so that this process can occur over time.

PRINCIPLE SEVEN: ADMINISTRATIVE COLLABORATION

Because in a constructive classroom environment, teachers and children constitute a community of learners, in a constructive working environment, teachers and administrators constitute a community of committed educational professionals. In an inservice education context which promotes such a community, school administrators can become more effective leaders because they are also learners and risk-takers. Teachers and administrators can discuss substantive issues and professional readings, and together they can explore instructional and institutional concerns. Teachers and administrators who work together in these ways build common goals and visions.

PRINCIPLE EIGHT: SCHOOL–COMMUNITY PARTNERSHIPS

Inservice education that acknowledges partnerships between and among teachers, parents, school officials, and members of the community strengthens the ties between school, faculty, and community. Activities which encourage teachers to affirm the genuine and diverse concerns of parents for the education of their children can create and/or reinforce parents' involvement and interest in education. Partnerships of various kinds, including those with business leaders, funding agencies, school boards, state departments of education, universities, and legislators, strengthen the ability of the school and its faculty to recognize and address the concerns of the larger community and to benefit from a richer and more substantial awareness of the contexts in which teaching and learning occur.

PRINCIPLE NINE: PLURALISM AND DEMOCRACY

Inservice education respects the cultural diversity of a school's community context and takes into account the needs and concerns of members of those cultures. By doing so, inservice education recognizes that teachers learn how to work effectively with students from many cultures in order to build genuine democratic communities in their classrooms and in our society. Whatever its focus, inservice education which is built on all these principles and continues to critique and revise them, provides genuine cases of teachers participating in a democracy and demonstrates to learners and others in the educational community how such participation sustains democratic values.

PRINCIPLE TEN: EXPLICIT AND TANGIBLE SUPPORT

Because participating in inservice education is a form of professional service to teachers' schools and students, districts must endorse teachers' continuing efforts to be involved in such education. Because through inservice education teachers are more likely to grow professionally, such participation must be recognized and supported. Tangible support—like compensation, reduced teaching responsibilities, funds for professional membership and travel, and allocation of released time—to engage in inservice education communicates to the entire educational community that such professional growth is an expected part of being a teacher.

CLOSING

These principles are intended to be general: to apply to all inservice education for teachers at all levels and in all disciplines and for all others in the school community. Our sense of professional growth demands that all experience such an approach. It is the case, however, that these principles spring from an understanding of teaching and learning which grows directly from the theorized practice of English language arts teachers and their students. So although these principles are by no means limited to teachers of the English language arts, they are drawn from and are consistent with what we understand of learning and teaching in language education.

Continuing Issues in the Preparation of English Language Arts Teachers

NCTE's Standing Committee on Teacher Preparation and Certification has developed these *Guidelines* by drawing upon the best knowledge base and the best practice that informs the profession at this time. To do this, it has been necessary to move beyond any one philosophical or pedagogical position or any one of the various competing researcher, practitioner, or "knowledge maker" groups of the sort discussed by Stephen North (1987). The result of this broad-based approach is that the ideas of many diverse groups—cognitivists, expressivists, constructionists, and others—contribute to the knowledge base supporting these *Guidelines*. Thus, the committee's view has much in common with that of Schallert (1991) who, in commenting on the debate between the cognitive approach and the social interactive approach to the teaching of writing, suggests that our students might best be served when we consider broadly "the psychological process of how individuals represent to themselves, and are influenced by, the social context in which writing occurs" (36).

We also agree with Greene (1986), who asserts that pedagogy must be morally defensible and that students as free agents must be respected. She contends that if individuals are to come to know or share meanings, they must be viewed as having the ability to think for themselves, and that "the kinds of conditions necessary for such thinking can be created in classrooms" (487). In order to create such classrooms, teachers must have a strong academic background in the English language arts, and the academic performance of their students must remain central to teaching and learning. Preservice teachers must also understand the larger context in which learning takes place. As Schallert writes:

> When students are learning about their language, when they are engaged in writing at the request of their teachers, when they are exploring their response to literature, they place themselves in uniquely vulnerable positions. Classroom systems and teacher responses,

unless carefully designed and humanely thoughtful, can easily crush their personal investments and future motivation to engage fully in these learning situations. (1991, p. 37)

How do we help our students attain both the highest levels of academic performance and the attitudes that accompany such learning? This question defines our basic mission in developing these *Guidelines*. To help answer it, we identify several issues that deserve continuing discussion among English language arts professionals.

1. Breadth of reference.

The 1996 *Guidelines* contains language and terminology from a wide range of professional and political points of view; for example, "expressive," "construction," "transactional," and "diversity." However, we avoid associating such terms with specific movements and schools of thought, and do not name, elaborate, or recommend specific conceptual frameworks. We did this deliberately to acknowledge the breadth of the knowledge base for English education and to avoid being over-prescriptive of the content in English teacher education programs. Thus, the guidelines refer only generally to the structures that inform the accreditation process, because we prefer to leave interpretive decisions to the discretion of individual programs, believing that such decisions must be situated in a local context (see, for example, the earlier chapter, "Characteristics of Effective Teacher-Preparation Programs for English Language Arts").

The broad reference base in these *Guidelines* arises from the Standing Committee's fundamental intention to produce a document based on the principle and spirit of inclusion. For example, this inclusiveness would lead to choosing texts from what has come to be called the traditional literary "canon" of British, world, and American literature, as well as oral and written texts from outside the canon, including English translations of texts originally written in other languages.

The breadth of reference in the *Guidelines* may also create the impression that the document is intended to be all things to all people. This is not the case. Instead, we wish to emphasize our belief that the diverse conceptual frameworks that inform English education share important common ground in terms of both theory and practice. Even though, for example, fundamental differences do separate social constructionists and expressivists, both groups jointly support a variety of teaching practices, especially those that center instruction on real rhetorical situations and those that bring students into active contact with a wide range of texts and audiences.

2. Common ground for the knowledge guidelines.

The knowledge guidelines articulated in this document are broadly conceived and rest on the common ground shared by various literary, rhetorical, and linguistic theories. For example, the guideline for language development includes an item based on a cognitivist point of view that focuses on the development of thought and language in individuals. That section, as well as other sections, also refers to a social constructionist perspective. Additionally, the guidelines on composing language and written discourse are primarily expressivist in their orientation, while the guideline on reading and literature refers to Louise

Rosenblatt's "transactional" theory of literature as well as to a more general reader-response approach to literary texts.

The knowledge guidelines demonstrate directly the Standing Committee's determination to draw attention to the importance of seeking commonalities among diverse, sometimes opposed, theories and their attendant practices. For programs seeking accreditation, this pluralistic, inclusionary approach leaves open many areas for interpretation. First, how should teachers approach translating such a variety of conceptual frameworks into coherent classroom practices, course plans, and programs? Second, how should programs be structured in order to reflect the broad and eclectic range of conceptual frameworks brought together in the *Guidelines*? Third, what range of options does such a pluralistic approach provide for teacher education programs to account for local and regional variations in culture, language, and dialect? Fourth, what range of options does such an approach leave open to programs beyond the implementation of superficial "survey" methods courses (Smagorinsky and Whiting, 1995)?

3. Balance between conservation and reform.

To what extent should each ten-year revision of the *Guidelines* reflect current professional and political trends and movements, and to what extent should the *Guidelines* express continuity with previous revisions?

One way of looking at the document as it has developed over the years is to see it as a cumulative, evolving text with its own characteristics, priorities, and language. In such a view, this is a conserving document that gives English educators the opportunity to focus their attention on disciplinary history and to maintain contact with long-held values. Such a view also encourages English educators to maintain contact with language and terminology that have helped define central disciplinary concerns and practices. For example, successive revisions of the *Guidelines* have used words like "process," "content," "media," and "discourse" that all English educators are able to recognize and relate to specific issues and classroom practices.

Another way of looking at the *Guidelines* is as a document that defines and redefines the discipline at regular ten-year intervals, and that responds to the professional, social, and political trends that are most significant during the time in which each revision is being composed. In such a view, *Guidelines for the Preparation of Teachers of English Language Arts* is an activist document which seeks change and attempts periodic reorientation of the discipline and the language used to represent it.

Both of these views lead to important insights, though neither view is sufficient in itself. Looking at the *Guidelines* in terms of its continuity with the past can lead to stagnation, reduction, and reification of language and practice. Looking at the *Guidelines* in the context of current trends and movements, on the other hand, leads to short-sightedness, excess, and distortion. Also, both of these views operating independently and unmindfully of each other in the discipline contribute to the so-called "swinging pendulum" effect. This phenomenon (which is not unique to English education) is characterized by oscillations in the orientation of the discipline from one extreme position to another. One example of this occurred during the 1940s and 1950s, in the years leading up to the collapse of the Progressive Movement. During that period, English educators strongly supported the "life adjustment curriculum" which rejected traditional practice based on academic study and invested single-mindedly in Progressive reform. The long-term result of this well-meaning, highly student-centered orientation was a de-emphasis of academic study and an embarrassingly weak curriculum that was discarded in favor of an "academic model" in the 1950s and 1960s. At the time, the academic model was interpreted as a reestablishment of traditional academic values that had been wrongly abandoned during the preceding period of reform. This model, in turn, led to a discipline-centered curriculum that ultimately also fell victim to its own excesses by failing to respond to the needs and interests of students. That academic model was swept aside in the turbulent political climate of the late 1960s and early 1970s (Applebee, 1974). In terms of this pattern, the current revision of the *Guidelines* suggests movement in the direction of many basic progressive principles, such as student-centeredness, expressive writing, and multiculturalism, without aligning itself with any particular movement or school of thought.

This basic tendency notwithstanding, the Standing Committee has made an earnest attempt through this revision of the *Guidelines* to seek explicitly and openly a balance between conservation and reform, a balance which would encourage teacher educators to develop ways in which academic rigor and student-centeredness will complement and not exclude each other. It would be impossible to argue that successive revisions of the *Guidelines* should not reflect changes in social, political, and professional circumstances. Such changes are, after all, at the heart of the revision process itself. It would be just as impossible to argue that any good would be served by any revision of the *Guidelines* which would dislodge the discipline from its traditions and underpinnings. Such balance is particularly important since *Guidelines for the Preparation of Teachers of English Language Arts* is used as a working document in the accreditation of English teacher education programs, which serve broad and varied communities and exist in bureaucratic institutions which, by their very nature, are often difficult and slow to change.

4. Conceptual frameworks.

In the 1996 revision, as was the case in the 1986 edition, the guidelines for pedagogy are firmly rooted in the process pedagogy of the 1980s. These guidelines highlight "learning/teaching processes" and refer frequently to such phenomena as mind-engaging processes, process measures, and meaning-making processes. Along with this emphasis on process there is, as there always has been in process pedagogy itself, a corresponding emphasis on the connections between individual cognitive development and teaching methods.

This stand on cognitivism and process pedagogy constitutes a strong link with previous revisions of the *Guidelines* while not overlooking the work of literary scholars, educational theorists, and rhetoricians who see themselves as representatives of more explicitly postmodern points of view such as social constructionism. This latter orientation posits a "liberatory" role as well as vigorous social activism for teachers of "literacy." Social constructionists also often operate on the basis of a broader "anti-foundationalist" agenda against what they understand to be the "foundational" tenets of cognitivism and process pedagogy. Despite these very real areas of disagreement, with respect to both the pedagogy guidelines and the knowledge guidelines, the Standing Committee strongly encourages programs seeking accreditation to emphasize connectedness and common ground across conceptual frameworks that often seem, on the surface, to be contradictory. These connections are important, especially given the fact that many teaching practices, such as authentic assessment and the use of reading and writing workshops, are central to enacting several different conceptual frameworks in the classroom.

5. New technologies.

As teacher educators look forward to preservice teachers' needs for the twenty-first century, they should be aware of the possibilities that new technologies offer. This revision of the *Guidelines* represents what the Standing Committee knows and was able to articulate about emerging technologies during the three-year period in which this edition was written. The use of the Internet, as one example, increased significantly even as we worked on this document. Graphic interfaces such as the World Wide Web have created additional possibilities for delivery of instruction, expansion of materials and resources, and interaction among diverse populations. As such interactive structures are developed for classrooms, the instructional uses of such technology need to be closely monitored. Teachers need to be knowledgeable about possible uses and abuses, especially as technology replaces more traditional teaching approaches.

Similarly, teachers must look carefully at the ways in which developments in learning and brain research inform pedagogy and attitudes. Technology is making it possible to literally monitor brain activity and learning over time. Educators are benefiting from that knowledge, but the misuse of it could cause effective teaching and learning to be called obsolete before there is sufficient information to make that judgment.

6. Educational reform.

The pedagogy guidelines focus attention on the many disparities among the *Guidelines*, teacher education programs, and language arts programs in secondary schools. Specifically, the pedagogy guidelines point out that the kinds of classrooms and teaching approaches represented in the *Guidelines* as a whole may differ substantially from current practices in the secondary schools and classrooms where beginning teachers will student teach and begin their careers. By drawing attention to these disparities, the Standing Committee acknowledges that one function of the *Guidelines* is to help initiate reform by educating teachers and then placing them in schools as agents of change. In this context, it is worth noting that even though many organizations and individual reformers have made similar attempts over the last one hundred years, educational historians like Cremin (1961) and Cuban (1993) argue that such reform efforts have had mixed success. Is this because classroom teachers are unwilling to change? Does it suggest a greater-than-understood degree of inertia in the public schools? Or does it indicate a serious and long-running estrangement of scholars, university teacher education programs, and accreditation authorities from the needs and desires of teachers, local communities, and their schools?

By continuing to encourage reform, the Standing Committee asserts its belief that preservice teacher education does have an effect on school policies and teaching practices, and that the fundamental student-centered principles that have guided the work of the National Council of Teachers of English over the last several decades still represent strongly held values in English education.

7. Sensitivity to student needs.

The section on attitudes stresses the importance of teachers developing an awareness and appreciation of students' backgrounds, language, and needs as learners. The need for such attitudes has been prominent in earlier versions of the *Guidelines* as well as in positions NCTE has taken since its founding in 1911 (particularly during periods like the late 1940s and early 1950s, and the late 1960s and early 1970s). Furthermore, such sensitivities toward students reflect long-standing commitment to tolerance and compassion for all individuals.

The attitudes section also affirms the need for English teachers to ground their attitudes toward the profession in ongoing scholarly practice. This practice should be reflected in teachers' efforts to establish challenging and rigorous lessons, courses, units, and programs of academic study. There must be strong guidance to encourage English teachers to design curricula and classroom approaches which challenge students to the highest level of academic excellence in English, enabling them to think and use language, to fully develop as individuals, and to interact successfully with others in the world. At the same time, English teachers must not overlook the context in which they foster high academic standards; these standards can be better achieved if they are based on the students' interests and are maintained in a setting that supports students and encourages universal respect.

In order to accomplish such complex tasks, it is necessary for English educators to understand that, ultimately, the shape that educational programs and approaches to teaching take depends strongly on the needs and wishes of the communities in which schools are located. Indeed, because it is often so difficult to balance rigorous academic standards with student-centered approaches, it is necessary for English educators and classroom teachers to develop an open and responsive understanding of local communities and a strong working relationship with school patrons and parents of current students (see Moffett, 1994).

REFERENCES

Applebee, A. N. (1974). *Tradition and reform in the teaching of English: A history.* Urbana, IL: National Council of Teachers of English.

Cremin, L. A. (1961). *The transformation of the school: Progressivism in American education, 1876–1957.* New York: Alfred A. Knopf.

Cuban, L. (1993). *How teachers taught: Constancy and change in American classrooms, 1890–1990* (2nd ed.). New York: Teachers College Press.

Greene, M. (1986). Philosophy and teaching. In M.C. Wittrock (Ed.), *Handbook of research on teaching* (3rd ed.), pp. 479–501. New York: Macmillan.

Moffett, J. (1994). *The universal schoolhouse: Spiritual awakening through education.* San Francisco: Jossey-Bass.

North, S. M. (1987). *The making of knowledge in composition: Portrait of an emerging field.* Upper Montclair, NJ: Boynton/Cook.

Schallert, D. L. (1991). The contribution of psychology to teaching the language arts. In J. Flood, J. M. Jensen, D. Lapp, and J. R. Squire (Eds.), *Handbook of research on teaching the English language arts,* pp. 30–39. New York: Macmillan.

Smagorinsky, P., & Whiting, M. E. (1995). *How English teachers get taught: Methods of teaching the methods class.* Urbana, IL: National Council of Teachers of English.

Appendix:
A Personal View from a Beginning Teacher

by Larry Crapse
English Coordinator, Florence Public School District One, South Carolina

On my first day of work as a high school English teacher, the principal held a brief meeting with all new faculty and told us emphatically that we were responsible for finding out what to do and how and when to do it. After making a few cryptic comments about how glad he was to have us on his staff, he exited the room to attend to "other pressing duties." Collectively stunned, the other teachers and I sat in uncomfortable silence for a few moments, having expected more direction from our leader. Finally, one gentleman cleared his throat and said, "I think it's time we made some new friends around here."

While my experience probably is not typical of most new English teachers, I did learn from it. I quickly realized that new teachers need older, more seasoned mentors to show them the ropes, to help them acquire the tacit knowledge necessary about the school and how it operates. Without such direction, the critical first year of classroom work might, for many teachers, be unpleasant at best, disastrous at worst.

I was fortunate to be befriended my first day on the job by a science teacher–football coach who methodically and patiently explained to me the procedures for acquiring books, setting up clerical records, securing necessary supplies, and handling the paperwork stuffed in my mailbox. In an informal but informative tour of the building and grounds, he gave me advice on how to deal with the front office, how to communicate with parents, how to deal with student discipline. In less than two hours, I had gained valuable insights into the culture of the school and its day-to-day operation. Because of this veteran teacher's kindness and generosity, I was able to prepare well for the opening of school and to feel that I had a friend to turn to in moments of confusion or uncertainty.

Over the course of my career, I have heard stories similar to mine—stories about how mentorship helped to make a smooth path out of a potentially rocky one during the first year. On the other hand, I have also heard from teachers who recalled with pain and regret the difficulties of their initial year of teaching, working without a mentor. Those unfortunate and disappointing experiences would not have occurred if other teachers had shown interest.

Veteran teachers can help their first-year colleagues in six simple, yet significant, ways. I believe experienced teachers should:

1. Go to the new teachers right away.

Don't wait for trouble to develop before acting. Let your presence and availability be known. Remember that new teachers may be too intimidated, shy, or overwhelmed to ask for help. A simple "I'm here if you need me" can mean the difference between desperation and success.

2. Offer practical advice.

Share with new teachers your most effective methods for getting things done. Let them in on your "secrets" for expediting requests, acquiring materials and resources, and handling students' problems and parents' concerns. Open to your new colleagues the files of written materials that you've developed to deal with these matters.

3. Be positive!

Let the new teachers know that you are interested in their work. Stop by their rooms briefly to see how they are doing, and congratulate them on what they have accomplished. Put little notes in their mailboxes when you hear or see something good they have done.

4. Show genuine concern and empathy.

Tell them what you have learned from your experience about particular problems they may be experiencing or feelings they may be expressing. The first year can be stressful; help it go more smoothly by lending a caring ear. Convey the impression that you are all part of a team working for the good of the students and the community. Demonstrate how looking beyond the walls of the classroom to the broader dimensions of the profession can be inspiring and renewing.

5. Respect the new teachers' space.

Keep in mind that these individuals are feeling pressures from many directions. Don't impose by offering too much advice, especially when it is unsolicited. Keep yourself at a comfortable but civilized distance as the year goes along. The first year is, in many ways, the most experimental. The teachers will undoubtedly appreciate your being near when needed.

6. Listen!

When the new teachers need someone to talk with, be willing to hear them out. Stop what you are doing, make eye contact, and use body language that shows your concern and interest. Never appear as if your thoughts are on some other topic. You may be able to give valuable advice, but remember that new teachers sometimes need another person simply to listen. Just being there may be enough.

Experienced teachers who follow these suggestions can help make a neophyte's first year of teaching more pleasant and successful. More important, though, such actions are evidence that teaching is more than just a job—it is a humanitarian effort that involves the best that lies within us, not only for our students but also for those who teach them.